one day
at a time

A 60-Day Challenge to See, Serve, and
Celebrate the People around You

kyle idleman

BakerBooks
a division of Baker Publishing Group
Grand Rapids, Michigan

© 2022 by Kyle Idleman

Published by Baker Books
a division of Baker Publishing Group
PO Box 6287, Grand Rapids, MI 49516-6287
www.bakerbooks.com

Printed in the United States of America

Library of Congress Cataloging-in-Publication Data
Names: Idleman, Kyle, author.
Title: One day at a time : A 60-day challenge to see, serve, and celebrate the people around you / Kyle Idleman.
Description: Grand Rapids, MI : Baker Books, a division of Baker Publishing Group, [2022]
Identifiers: LCCN 2022006497 | ISBN 9781540902405 (cloth) | ISBN 9781493437801 (ebook)
Subjects: LCSH: Devotional calendars. | Interpersonal relations—Religious aspects—Christianity—Miscellanea. | Change—Religious aspects—Christianity—Miscellanea.
Classification: LCC BV4811 .I35 2022 | DDC 242/.2—dc23/eng/20220315
LC record available at https://lccn.loc.gov/2022006497

Unless otherwise indicated, Scripture quotations are from THE HOLY BIBLE, NEW INTERNATIONAL VERSION®, NIV® Copyright © 1973, 1978, 1984, 2011 by Biblica, Inc.® Used by permission. All rights reserved worldwide.

Scripture quotations labeled ESV are from The Holy Bible, English Standard Version® (ESV®), copyright © 2001 by Crossway, a publishing ministry of Good News Publishers. Used by permission. All rights reserved. ESV Text Edition: 2016

Scripture quotations labeled Message are from THE MESSAGE, copyright © 1993, 2002, 2018 by Eugene H. Peterson. Used by permission of NavPress. All rights reserved. Represented by Tyndale House Publishers, Inc.

Scripture quotations labeled NLT are from the Holy Bible, New Living Translation, copyright © 1996, 2004, 2007, 2013, 2015 by Tyndale House Foundation. Used by permission of Tyndale House Publishers, Inc., Carol Stream, Illinois 60188. All rights reserved.

Portions of this text have been adapted from One at a Time (Baker Books, 2022).

Some names and details have been changed to protect the privacy of the individuals involved.

Published in association with the literary agent Don Gates of The Gates Group, www.the-gates-group.com.

Baker Publishing Group publications use paper produced from sustainable forestry practices and post-consumer waste whenever possible.

22 23 24 25 26 27 28   7 6 5 4 3 2 1

contents

contents

WEEK 7

the practice of celebrating
[one party at a time]

WEEK 8

the practice of weighing words
[one word at a time]

WEEK 1

the practice of
noticing

[zoom lens]

what do you see?

THE CROWDS PUSHED IN all around her. Dozens of voices shouting so close her ears rang with their pleas and demands. Everyone wanted something from the man walking past.

She managed to catch glimpses of him between all the shoulders and was surprised to see he looked very ordinary. The way the crowd gravitated toward him suggested anything but that. Heart pounding against her rib cage, she knew her last chance at healing the sickness that had taken so much from her was about to walk past unless she did something.

A sliver of space between two people opened up, and she quickly slipped between them. Now nothing separated her from the Son of God but the distance of an arm's length. Awe at being this close to Jesus almost stopped her in her tracks, but the hope swelling in her chest urged her forward. She knew if she could just touch him, she would be healed, and so faith propelled her. She reached out and managed to just skim the edge of his cloak.

It was enough. Immediately, she knew. The constant bleeding was gone. Overcome with relief, she barely heard the voice that spoke over the crowd.

"Who touched me?" the voice asked. "I felt the power go out of me." *Oh no.* Her breath caught in her throat as she looked up and met Jesus's eyes.

But the men surrounding him, his disciples, laughed incredulously at his question. "You see the people crowding against you; it could have been anyone," they said.

Jesus continued to lock eyes with her and, as seconds that felt like minutes ticked by, she realized she couldn't go unnoticed. Fear shook her small frame as she hesitantly walked to him and fell at his feet.

"I-I was the one who touched you." She couldn't look him in the eyes as she spoke. "And now I am healed."

Jesus's gentle voice soothed her nerves as he said loud enough for everyone to hear, "Daughter, your faith has healed you. Go in peace and be freed from your suffering" (see Mark 5:24–34).

QUESTION: Who has God put in your life who needs healing? If no one comes to mind, pray until someone does. How could you touch that person in a way that might relieve some of their suffering and possibly point them to Jesus?

CHALLENGE: One thing we tend to notice is . . . our phones. So, how about every time you touch your phone today, you say a quick prayer for a hurting person you can touch with Jesus's love?

2

what do you want to see?

WE SEE WHAT WE WANT TO SEE.

Psychologists have a term for that: *motivated perception.* The idea is we don't see everything. What we notice is biased and selective.

You may have heard of your *reticular activating system.* No? Here's the scientific, super-nerdy definition:

The reticular activating system (RAS) is a network of neurons located in the brain stem that project anteriorly to the hypothalamus to mediate behavior, as well as both posteriorly to the thalamus and directly to the cortex for activation of awake, desynchronized cortical EEG patterns.*

*"Reticular Activating System," Science Direct, accessed March 14, 2022, https://www.sciencedirect.com/topics/veterinary-science-and -veterinary-medicine/reticular-activating-system.

Do you get that? Me neither! But here's what I do know: the reticular activating system is your brain's gatekeeper of information. It leads you to ignore what you've predecided is nonessential and notice what you consider important.

This is why you never noticed a silver Honda Pilot until you started thinking about buying one. Then you were seeing silver Honda Pilots everywhere. Were they there before? Yep, your brain was just choosing to ignore them. You didn't notice them until they became important to you.

So, let me ask: What do you see in your home? When you're driving? At work? At the grocery store? On the sidelines at your kids' games? Walking through your neighborhood?

What do you see?

You see what you're looking for, what's important to you, what you've trained your eyes to see.

I bet you'd be stunned by what you *don't* see: that there are all kinds of hurting people God puts in your path.

I asked what you see. How about this: What did Jesus see? Forty times in the Gospels we read, "Jesus saw." Those two words are the launching point of so many amazing stories of transformed lives.

If we want to have the results Jesus had—those amazing stories—we need to see what Jesus saw.

What did Jesus see?

He saw hurting people, desperate people, people who needed God. Why is that what he saw? Because that's what he was looking for; that's what was important to him.

QUESTION: Think back on the last couple of days. Who might God have put in your path—so you might love them and point them to Jesus—but you didn't notice or just ignored them? Ask God to bring those people to mind.

CHALLENGE: Start beginning your day with the prayer, "God, help me to see what you want me to see." Ask God to give you his eyes for hurting people who need him.

what Jesus saw

THE MOVIE *SAW* came out in 2004. *Saw II* followed in 2005. In 2006 came *Saw III*. In 2007, *Saw IV*, and 2008 saw the release of *Saw V. Saw VI* came out in 2009. Then, in 2010, *Saw: The Final Chapter.*

What's my point? Well, putting out a movie every year is a lot for a film series. Also, there wasn't a lot of creativity in titling those movies. But mostly . . . in seven years there were seven *Saw* movies.

Is that important? Not at all. But in Matthew 9, the word *saw* occurs seven times.

Seven *Saws*. Seven "saws."

Kind of cool.

Anyhoo . . . while reading Matthew 9, I noticed *saw* kept appearing. Seven times we read about what someone saw. And that's not to mention the two blind men who couldn't see but then could. Reading the chapter, I realized I wouldn't have seen what Jesus did.

At the beginning of the chapter, some men brought to Jesus a paralyzed man. What would I have seen? Well, duh. A paralyzed man. But what about Jesus? "When Jesus saw their faith . . ." (v. 2).

Also interesting: Jesus told the man his sins were forgiven rather than his legs were healed. He saw a need in the man's life that wouldn't have been my focus in that moment.

Then Jesus turned to the religious leaders, whom I would've ignored, and told them what they were thinking, which I could never have seen either.

Next, we're told, "As Jesus went on from there, he saw a man named Matthew sitting at the tax collector's booth" (v. 9). I would've looked at Matthew and seen a traitor, a Jewish man working for the occupying, oppressive Roman government. Jesus saw his next disciple. "'Follow me,' he told him, and Matthew got up and followed him" (v. 9).

Matthew then threw a party for his friends to meet Jesus and, we're told, "When the Pharisees saw this, they asked his disciples, 'Why does your teacher eat with tax collectors and sinners?'" (v. 11). They saw Jesus eating with the wrong people. I wonder if that's what I would've seen. Jesus replied, "It is not the healthy who need a doctor, but the sick" (v. 12). What he saw were people who needed spiritual healing.

In verse 20 a sick woman fought through a crowd to get to Jesus and touch his cloak for healing. The disciples saw only the crowd. I'm afraid that's exactly what I would've seen too. But in the jumbled mass of the crowd, "Jesus turned and saw her" (v. 22).

Next, Jesus got to a home where people were weeping and wailing for a little girl who just died. Jesus "saw the noisy crowd" (v. 23) and then went in to the girl. If I were with him, I would've seen a dead girl. Jesus saw her as asleep, and he "took the girl by the hand, and she got up" (v. 25).

Jesus left there and started traveling through towns and villages filled with people. We're told,

> When he saw the crowds, he had compassion on them, because they were harassed and helpless, like sheep without a shepherd. Then he said to his disciples, "The harvest is plentiful but the workers are few. Ask the Lord of the harvest, therefore, to send out workers into his harvest field." (vv. 36–38)

I would've seen an overwhelming amount of people. I might have been tempted to condemn some. Jesus looked at them through eyes of compassion, seeing them as people who needed their heavenly Father and as a potential harvest.

I read all that and realize I have broken eyes. It breaks my heart. No wonder I haven't had the impact I want to.

I pray God will heal my eyes the way he healed the legs of the paralyzed man. I pray he will wake my sleeping heart and give me new life the way he did for the little girl.

QUESTION: What do you think is the most common thing you don't see in people's lives? What are you missing that Jesus would see?

CHALLENGE: Today, each time you look at a person, ask, "But Jesus, what do you see?" Pray you'll have his eyes of compassion and see beyond the surface to the pain and need of that person.

the secret way

IN THE MID-1990S, there were pictures with patterns in which, if you looked at them just right, a 3D image would appear.

I had a buddy in my neighborhood who had two or three of these "magic" pictures hanging in his house. He thought they were really cool. He invited me over and immediately wanted to show them to me. Several minutes passed of me gazing at the pictures. I looked with my eyes narrow then wide, from one angle then another, from up close then at a distance. Nothing seemed to do the trick.

"Can you see it?" My friend asked, practically bouncing on his feet with excitement.

"No, I don't see anything!" I snapped at him.

A few seconds passed.

"How about now?" he asked. "Can you see it now? You've got to really want to see it!"

My eyes were watering from not blinking for so long, but I still didn't see "it." Eventually I was sweating, feeling a little lightheaded and defeated. I told my friend I gave up. I decided it was either a practical joke or my friend was smoking something. (In hindsight, my friend may have been smoking something.)

I turned around as we were walking out of the room and glared at the picture. I decided to make one last-ditch effort. My eyes practically popping out of my head, I thought to myself, *Don't blink, Kyle. Just look. Stare at it just right. You can do this.* Suddenly a sailboat in the clouds emerged from the picture.

"I see it! I see it!" I shouted at my friend, and we both started hollering in triumph. I'd been looking at it and looking at it and couldn't see the image. But then when I saw it, it was all I could see.

Going back to the story of the woman whom Jesus healed in Mark 5, let's focus on verse 30, when Jesus asked the crowd, "Who touched my clothes?" His question seemed nonsensical. There were dozens of people surrounding him and bumping into him. But Jesus asked the question because he always saw things other people didn't seem to notice. One of the secrets of his amazing influence is that he noticed the overlooked.

When we examine Jesus's one at a time lifestyle, we find that everything he did was intentional. The only way to see the image of the sailboat emerge from the messy pattern was to look intentionally at the picture. Jesus asked the question of "who" and suddenly, out of the messy swarm of people in front of him, a woman appeared. She was no longer a part of the crowd. She was an individual with a unique story and a specific need. She was God's daughter.

QUESTION: When was the last time you asked the "who" question and thought about a specific person's needs and how you could meet them? So, who? Who needs help, encouragement, a warm meal, a kind note, a hug?

CHALLENGE: Today you're going to see lots of people. They may look like a crowd. Ask God "who" and try to meet someone's need. Do something kind for them that may inconvenience you but might make their day.

a new lens

IN THE THIRD GRADE, I started having trouble in class. No matter how hard I tried, I just couldn't keep up with the other students or with my homework. Both my teacher and parents were quick to assume it was because I struggled with focusing. My report cards all said the same things: "Kyle doesn't sit still. He doesn't listen to or follow directions." This was such an established issue that when my grades started declining, it was the go-to assumption.

In class, my teachers gave me lectures on paying closer attention. When my performance didn't improve, privileges were taken away from me. But it just kept getting worse.

Eventually, my dad decided it was probably because I just wasn't all that smart. Well, he never *actually* said that to me, but he did tell me, "Son, I'm just as proud of your Cs as your sister's As, as long as you're trying your best."

While all this was going on, I went to the eye doctor for the first time in my life. When the eye chart was put in front of me, I had a hard time deciphering the different letters and numbers. Then the doctor set a big contraption in front of my face and had me look through different lenses he flipped through. Finally, everything came into focus as I looked through one of the lenses.

I was very soon the owner of a pair of unfortunate Clark Kent–meets–Sally Jessie Raphael glasses. The next day at school, while the other kids were making fun of me for wearing glasses that were slightly bigger than my entire head, I discovered I could read the chalkboard. It turned out it wasn't my effort, my intellect, or my ADD that was the problem.

The problem was that I needed to see the world through a new set of lenses.

When Jesus asked, "Who touched me?" in Mark 5, the disciples couldn't believe their ears. They asked him in verse 31, "You see the people crowding against you . . . and yet you can ask, 'Who touched me?'" In that moment, the disciples looked at the people through a crowd lens, seeing them as distractions and disruptions. They wanted Jesus to just shrug his shoulders and keep moving, to dismiss one person's need because there were so many others piling up.

What they needed was to put on Jesus's one at a time lens so they would stop seeing people as inconveniences but instead as God-given opportunities to love and meet needs.

QUESTION: Do you see the people around you as inconveniences or opportunities? When is the last time you dismissed someone because they couldn't do anything for you in return or because you just didn't have time for them?

CHALLENGE: Ask God to help you look at the people around you through a new lens. With that transformed outlook, go out of your way (today, or tomorrow at the latest) to stop and have a conversation with someone you normally wouldn't notice. It can be as simple as asking them about their day.

WEEK 2

the practice of
processing

[*in then through*]

the right way to start

WE DON'T KNOW MUCH about Jesus's first thirty years.

But then he stepped onto the public stage and declared who he was and what he had come to do.

Then Jesus was baptized. At his baptism, God spoke from heaven, affirming Jesus was his Son.

And then . . .

Jesus went off, into the wilderness, all by himself, and prayed for forty days.

That's commendable. But it's also kind of weird. Right? Think about it: Jesus announced he's starting his ministry. God spoke from heaven, "This is my Son!"

Everyone's excited. It's happening!

Then Jesus said, "I gotta go!" and went off by himself to pray for forty days.

That isn't typically the way you launch something you want to gain momentum, especially if you want it to become a worldwide movement and you've spent the first three decades of your life in obscurity. You don't go back into obscurity for six more weeks!

But Jesus did. He started his ministry with prayer. He went away to a place of silence so he could feel God's presence and pray. So he could breathe in God's love, hear God's whisper, talk to God, and access God's power.

Then . . . Jesus came back!

Okay. Here we go! *Let's get ready to rumble!*

Jesus started his ministry, and in Mark 1 we get a description of Jesus's first day on the job as the Messiah. We see Jesus teaching and healing people. It's a great beginning.

The day ended and Jesus went to sleep. He got up early the next day. Which I get. That's what I'd do too. There are so many more people to teach and heal. I'd be up early writing sermons and doing some stretching so I'd be ready to touch all the sick people.

Except that's *not* why Jesus got up early. Here's what he did: "Very early in the morning, while it was still dark, Jesus got up, left the house and went off to a solitary place, where he prayed" (Mark 1:35).

To be clear: Jesus went to a place of silence for a month and a half, then he came back, had one day of activity, and headed straight back to a place of silence so he could feel God's presence and pray.

We see Jesus do this over and over. It was the rhythm of his life. And not just Jesus's life but also the rhythm he established for his followers: "Then, because so many people were coming and going . . . he said to them, 'Come with me by yourselves to a quiet place'" (6:31).

Jesus used the word *abide*, which means "to live in." Jesus said he abided in his Father, and he invites us to abide in him. He said if we don't abide, we won't abound. If we don't prioritize our relationship with God, we can accomplish nothing of significance.

We have a hard time making the connection between getting up very early in the morning while it's still dark to pray and making a difference with our lives during the day. We focus on what we want God to do *through* us, but impact almost always follows the formula of in *then* through, and *in* almost always happens early in the morning while it's still dark.

So, how do you start a one at a time life? How do you live a high-impact Christlike life? You start with prayer. You get away to a place of silence so you can feel God's presence and pray.

QUESTION: How serious are you about prayer? Does your prayer life reveal a desperation for God's wisdom and power? Are you trying to do great things for God without God's help?

CHALLENGE: Take some time today to pray about your prayer life. Ask God to show you what needs to change.

planted and cultivated

ONE DAY I WAS CLEANING my house and found some seed packets. It triggered a memory from years earlier. An elderly lady at church had given me these watermelon and pumpkin seeds for Christmas. An unusual gift, but I'd been excited to grow them. I thought, *Hey, I like pumpkin pie. This will be fun!* I remember going home and googling how long it would take for the seeds to grow.

That was years ago. I never did anything with those seeds. I forgot about them after making the fateful mistake of placing them in a drawer. Not just any drawer; the *junk* drawer. You know the junk drawer—it's where things go to disappear. Apparently, it's also not an especially conducive environment for plant growth to take place.

I had the seeds, but unless I planted them in soil and cultivated them, there could be no growth and no harvest.

Where are those seeds today? I hate to admit it, but they're still in the junk drawer. From time to time, I have a craving for watermelon or pumpkin pie and I think, *Oh yeah, the seeds!* The problem is that in those moments I want an immediate harvest, but that's not how it works. Before the harvest there must be planting and cultivating.

In Matthew 13, Jesus told a parable about a farmer who scattered seed. Different seeds fell on different types of soil. Some fell on soil that was too hard or too shallow, so the seed didn't sink in and take root. Other seeds fell on good soil and took root, growing and eventually producing a harvest.

Jesus used the metaphor of a seed because it's a great example of the *in then through* way that God works. God created seeds to create a harvest. He hardwired the end goal of the harvest into the seed, designing it so that with the right soil and the right conditions the seed would eventually bear fruit.

Sometimes people read this parable and think of themselves as the farmer. The farmer is the hero of the story. He's the one making things happen. But to be clear, in this parable *Jesus* is the farmer and we are the soil. He wants to bring a harvest through us, but he first must do his work *in* us.

Another mistake we make when reading this parable is focusing too much on the harvest when we first need to give our attention to the condition of the soil. Crops won't come *out of* the ground unless the right things first happen *in* the ground.

Unfortunately, what's happening in the ground is often easy to underestimate. We don't realize the harvest is the result of what's been happening in the soil. We overlook what's happening in the soil because we can't see it.

It's the fruit we can see and focus on.

You wouldn't be reading this book if you didn't want to live a fruitful life. You want to have influence in the lives of your friends and family members. You want to see your coworkers and neighbors come to faith. Fruit excites you. That's great, but fruit won't happen in your life unless planting and cultivating happen first.

Harvesting is fun and its reward is immediate, but what has to happen first, in the ground, is hard work.

When I give my attention to what God wants to do through me, I always discover that he first wants to do something in me. Philippians 2:13 says, "It is God who works in you," but why? The verse continues, "to will and to act in order to fulfill his good purpose."

QUESTION: How much time do you spend focused on and praying about fruit? ("God, help me to have an impact."

"Father, let me lead my friend to Jesus.") And how much time do you spend focused on being planted and cultivated? ("I need to get up early so I can spend some serious time praying." "Father, I know I can't lead my friend to Jesus without your help. Please help me.")

CHALLENGE: Tomorrow we're going to think about a plan for cultivation—creating a strategy for spiritual growth. Today, take a moment to write down your current plan. What are the things you intentionally and strategically do that help you to abide in and become more like Jesus? Write them down. Does your plan look like one that prioritizes spiritual cultivation?

creating a plan

IN CHAPTER 2 OF *ONE AT A TIME* we saw the examples of Mother Teresa and Linda Wilson-Allen, and how both of their fruitful lives began by prioritizing what God wanted to do *in* them. If you study the lives of godly, influential people, you see that's always the case.

John Wesley led an amazing, high-impact life for Jesus. We might see that and assume he was just more gifted than we are. But no; he was more *cultivated*. He prioritized what God wanted to do *in him* above what God wanted to do *through* him.

John Wesley taught that you plan for what is important to you. If you want to stop working someday, you make a retirement plan. If you really want to get in shape, you create a workout plan. And if you'd like to become more like Jesus, you put a spiritual growth plan in place. That's exactly what Wesley did.

During his time at Oxford University, he and some of his friends formed a small group to support and challenge each other to stick to their plan so they would grow spiritually.

Wesley's plan was very extensive. I'll just highlight four key elements.

- **Bible study and prayer.** John Wesley would typically spend four to nine hours a day in Bible study and prayer. He started at 4:00 a.m. Wow! Some days I do well to spend four to nine minutes. But Wesley was serious about his time of Bible study and prayer because he believed it was a big part of what empowered him to really know and become like Jesus.
- **Strict accountability.** He had several trusted people who asked him some tough questions every day.
- **Time management.** Wesley lived by the motto, "Every moment must be useful." He kept journals of how he used his time to see where he could improve.
- **Sacrificial giving.** He made a lot of money but continually gave it away.

One time Wesley came across a girl whose clothes were so worn they barely covered her body. It was obvious she hadn't eaten in a long time. In his journal he wrote that his heart leapt with joy when he saw her because God was giving him an opportunity to meet someone's need. He said to her, "I'm so excited for this chance to help you. I'm going to give you everything I have."

He reached into his pocket, but there was nothing in it. He cried all the way back to his house because he felt like he had been wasteful and it had resulted in having nothing to give this girl.

When he arrived at his house, he noticed two pictures on the wall, and he wept because he thought, *If I hadn't bought those pictures, I would have had something to give that girl.*

He encapsulated his theory about money by saying, "When I have money, I get rid of it quickly, lest it find a way into my heart." He was right. Jesus said, "Where your money is, there your heart is also" and, "You cannot love both God and money" (see Matt. 6:21; Luke 16:13). That's part of why the Bible teaches us to be generous in giving our money to God and to those in need. Because when we do, our money and our things lose their hold on us, and our hearts grow toward God.

You plan for what's important to you.

I read about John Wesley and get intimidated because I could never implement that intense of a plan in my life. But rather than letting Wesley's plan discourage me, I can let it inspire and stretch me. Maybe I couldn't live out his plan, but I can implement a better plan than what I have now. I can make sure that every day I am doing some intentional things that will help me become more like Jesus. I'm not going to spend four to nine hours a day in Bible study and prayer, but I could spend thirty minutes. I might not do accountability with another person every day, but I could do once a week.

We need to be cultivated. We need to give God space to work *in* us, because that will allow him to work *through* us in a bigger way than we've ever known.

QUESTION: How does hearing about John Wesley's plan for spiritual growth impact you?

CHALLENGE: Create a plan for your spiritual growth. What should it include? Bible study? Prayer? Accountability? Giving? What else? Make a plan that's ambitious but doable. You want it to stretch you but not be something impossible to live out so you become discouraged.

how *through* happens

WHEN I WAS A YOUNG PASTOR, I went to lunch with an older pastor who was an unofficial mentor of mine. He was impacting tens of thousands of people, and I wanted to ask him, "How do you do that?"

While we were eating, a woman came up and introduced herself. She told us about a need in her life and asked us to pray for her. We both said we would.

Confession time: it was a busy day. I forgot all about it.

More confession: that's not the only time I promised to pray for someone but forgot.

Later that week I stopped by this pastor's office, and I saw someone's name on a piece of paper taped above his desk, in a prominent place where he would see it. The name seemed familiar to me, so I asked him, "Where do I know that name from?"

He answered, "That's the lady we said we would pray for the other day."

Oh. That was the answer to my question. *That's how you impact thousands. You pray for them—one at a time.* We pray for them because we want to influence them but realize we can't on our own.

I love how David began Psalm 23: "The LORD is my shepherd." Just five words, but they say so much. If the Lord was David's shepherd, what did that make David? A sheep. That's not especially impressive or flattering.

Sheep are not intelligent. I read about a true story that came out of the town of Gevas, Turkey, in 2005. A flock of sheep was briefly left unattended by their shepherds. One walked off a cliff and fell to its death. Then 1,500 other sheep followed. The first 450 died, but as the pile grew higher the fall became more cushioned, so the other 1,050 survived.*

Sheep aren't capable of taking care of themselves and so are utterly dependent on a shepherd. When David—a former shepherd—started his psalm by saying, "I am not the shepherd. I am the sheep," it was a declaration of dependence.

We like to think, *I've got this. I can do this. I'm capable. My momma was right; I'm amazing.* But if we're going to have an impactful life, we need to admit: *I* don't *have this.*

*Associated Press, "450 Sheep Jump to Their Deaths in Turkey," *USA Today*, July 8, 2005, http://usatoday30.usatoday.com/news/offbeat/2005 -07-08-sheep-suicide_x.htm.

I can't do it. I'm not capable. I'm not the shepherd. I am the sheep. I am dependent.

The great news is that God will go with us and empower us if we engage in his mission.

When Jesus saw people who "were like sheep without a shepherd," his response was to ask his disciples to pray. "The harvest is plentiful but the workers are few. Ask the Lord of the harvest, therefore, to send out workers into his harvest field" (Matt. 9:36–38).

But he doesn't want them (or us) to just pray; he commanded them to *go*: "Therefore go and make disciples of all nations, baptizing them in the name of the Father and of the Son and of the Holy Spirit, and teaching them to obey everything I have commanded you" (28:19–20). He told them to go and promised to go with them (and us): "And surely I am with you always, to the very end of the age" (v. 20).

The apostle Paul dedicated his life to Jesus's mission and saw it as a divine partnership. I love how he wrote, "We are therefore Christ's ambassadors, as though God were making his appeal through us" (2 Cor. 5:20). He knew his responsibility was to represent Jesus and implore people to be reconciled to him, but he felt God empowering his efforts.

How do you impact thousands of people? You live in a way that represents Jesus well. You share Jesus in a compelling and compassionate way. But before God can do that through you, he has to do something in you. So, you pray—for each person you hope to impact—one at a time.

QUESTION: How much of your prayer time do you spend praying for people who are lost and need Jesus? How does that compare to the amount you spend praying for your own needs? What does that say?

CHALLENGE: Choose three people God has put in your life who are far from him. Commit to praying for those three people *at least* three times a week. Do something to make sure you don't forget—maybe put it in your phone calendar with reminder alerts or post their names on a note in a prominent place where you'll see it.

planted

BEFORE GOD CAN DO SOMETHING through you, he has to do something in you. God wants to produce a harvest through you, but that doesn't just happen. To understand one of the essentials for having a harvest, we need to go back to seeds.

God tells us in Psalm 92:12–15,

> The righteous will flourish like a palm tree,
>   they will grow like a cedar of Lebanon;
> planted in the house of the LORD,
>   they will flourish in the courts of our God.
> They will still bear fruit in old age,
>   they will stay fresh and green,
> proclaiming, "The LORD is upright;
>   he is my Rock, and there is no wickedness in him."

We can flourish like a cedar or a palm, which are both strong, durable trees that stay green all year long. They always flourish.

What kind of person flourishes like that? Those who are "planted in the house of the LORD, they will flourish in the courts of our God" (v. 13).

The image of being planted suggests we are seeds. A seed has incredible potential. Life exists within it. But a seed grows only if it's planted. If a seed doesn't get planted . . . it doesn't produce anything.

We are seeds. We need to be planted. Where? In the house of the Lord.

The house of the Lord is church.

A lot of people today are saying, "You know, I can be a Christian and not go to church." That may be true. But you can't be a *flourishing* Christian and not go to church.

For God to do all he wants to do in you, you need to go to church. Actually, you need to more than *go*; you need to get *planted* in church, in the house of the Lord. What does that look like?

First, a person who is planted never asks, "Are we going to church this week?" You know the conversation I'm talking about.

"Are we going to go to church tomorrow?"

"I don't know. I'm kind of tired. There's a game on. The kids have to . . ."

No, people who are planted don't ask. They go.

We never ask, "Are we going to eat today?" "Are we going to sleep tonight?" Of course we are. Eating and sleeping are essential to our physical lives, to our being healthy and flourishing physically. And church is essential to our spiritual lives, to our being healthy and flourishing spiritually.

Second, a person who is planted develops community in their church. They find a place—a small group, student ministry, Sunday school class—where they can share life with others, learn with them, and support each other.

Third, a person who is planted invests in their church. They give financially. They volunteer. They're not consumers. They don't show up and expect everyone else to serve them and pay the bill. Jesus has done so much in their lives, so they want to give back and make a difference for him.

If you get planted like that, you know what happens? You grow roots and fruits.

You don't see the roots, but they're the most important part of the tree. They provide the foundation. They take in the nutrients. The deeper the roots, the stronger the tree.

I read about redwood trees. They grow to three hundred feet high and thirty feet wide. How is that possible? Their roots. A redwood tree's roots go up to 150 feet down *and* out. The roots of each tree intertwine with the roots of the other redwood trees.

It's the same with people who flourish. You don't see their root system, but they have one. They've planted themselves in a church where they weave themselves together with other believers.

When you're planted, you also bear fruit. Remember Psalm 92 said, of those who are planted, "They will still bear fruit in old age, they will stay fresh and green" (v. 14), just like a healthy plant or tree. Fruit starts as the result of God's work *in* you. Galatians 5:22–23 tells us, "But the fruit of the Spirit is love, joy, peace, forbearance, kindness, goodness, faithfulness, gentleness and self-control." God transforms you from the inside out.

The fruit continues as God works *through* you. Paul referred to people who came to faith through his ministry as his fruit (see Rom. 1:13 and 1 Cor. 16:15 NLT). Being planted empowers you to live a one at a time life that grows into a harvest of people who find faith and fall in love with Jesus.

QUESTION: Are you planted in the house of the Lord? Do you attend a church consistently? Moreover, are you connected and invested in that church? If not, ask God to reveal to you how that might be part of the reason you're not seeing more fruit in your life.

CHALLENGE: One of the reasons God wants us connected in a church community is because it can help us to reach our friends for him. How could you take more of a "team approach" to loving and serving your unchurched friends? This week, come up with a way of introducing an unchurched friend to someone (or a group of someones) at your church in a way that might meet their need and point them to Jesus.

WEEK 3

the practice of
being
present

[the proximity principle]

the march

DID YOU SEE THE 2005 DOCUMENTARY *March of the Penguins*? It begins with the narrator saying,

> In some ways this is a story of survival, a tale of life over death. But it's more than that really; this is a story about love. . . . Like most love stories, it begins with an act of utter foolishness. The emperor penguin is technically a bird, although one that makes his home in the sea. So, if you're wondering what he's doing up here on the ice, well, that's part of our story. Each year, at around the same time, he will leave the comfort of his ocean home and embark on a remarkable journey. He will travel a great distance and though he is a bird he won't fly. Though he lives in the sea, he won't swim. Mostly, he will walk.[*]

As the movie continues, we learn that the walk of the emperor penguin is actually a march of love. He'll travel

[*]"Transcripts: March of the Penguins," CNN, accessed March 14, 2022, http://www.cnn.com/TRANSCRIPTS/1401/05/se.01.html.

seventy miles every year in temperatures ranging from 58 to 80 degrees *below zero*. The purpose of this march is to find love, to find a mate.

When most people think of Jesus, they think of the cross and how he died. And perhaps they think of Easter, how he rose from the grave. And so in some ways his is a story of survival, a tale of life over death.

But when you read the Gospels, you realize it's really a story about love. It begins with what seems an act of utter foolishness. Jesus leaves the comfort of heaven and embarks on a remarkable journey. He travels a great distance, and mostly, he walks. As the story continues, we learn that the walk of Jesus is actually a march of love. That he will travel any distance to, in a sense, find God a mate. We see Jesus repeatedly making his march of love.

For instance, we read that Jesus "left Judea and went back once more to Galilee. Now he had to go through Samaria" (John 4:3–4). This verse makes it sound like Jesus "had to go" through Samaria because of geographical necessity, but that wasn't it.

In fact, at the time the Jews and the Samaritans hated each other and would never enter each other's territory. Jewish people often made the trip from Judea to Galilee—but none took the direct route through Samaria. Instead, they would take a long detour around the Sea of Galilee. All because they wouldn't be caught dead in Samaria.

But Jesus, a Jew, "had to go through Samaria." Why? If it wasn't geography, what was it?

It was a woman. There was a woman in Samaria who had gone from man to man to man. She was living in guilt and shame. The men of her town loved to use her. The women loved to hate her.

So Jesus and his twelve disciples had to go into Samaria. Jesus was on a march of love. Jesus met the woman, and they proceeded to have a life-changing conversation. She finally met a man who could offer her the love she'd been searching for all her life.

Another time Jesus and his friends got in a boat and began traveling across a lake to the region of the Gerasenes (see Matt. 8:28–34). A storm came up and chaos erupted. Waves broke across the boat. Jesus's guys, several of whom were professional fishermen, were screaming, "We're going to drown!"

The only course of action that made sense was to turn around, but they didn't. It's like Jesus *had to go* to the region of the Gerasenes.

Finally, they arrived. They stayed there for only a short part of the day. During their stay, only one thing happened. Then they headed straight back.

What was so important it was worth risking their lives going through a storm to get to? A man. A man whose life was in complete turmoil. It was so bad, and he was considered so dangerous, that he was kept locked up in a cemetery far away from town. *He* was the reason.

Jesus was on a march of love. Jesus met the man, and they proceeded to have a life-changing conversation. This man finally met the One who could remove what had been tormenting him.

QUESTION: What is the farthest you've ever traveled, or the most inconvenienced you've ever been, to get close to and be present with someone who needs to experience God's love through you?

CHALLENGE: Pray about who God is calling you to connect with through a march of love. Whoever he puts on your mind, reach out to that person at least with a text or phone call—but if you can go to them in person, even better.

the power of proximity

IT'S HARD TO LOVE SOMEONE if we keep them at a distance. If we're following Jesus and loving people the way he did, it'll mean constantly being pointed to people who need us to point them to Jesus.

Philip powerfully demonstrated the priority of proximity. He was part of starting a new church and was leading a *revival*. We're told that many people were coming to faith and being baptized.

Then, in the midst of this,

> As for Philip, an angel of the Lord said to him, "Go south down the desert road that runs from Jerusalem to Gaza." So he started out. (Acts 8:26–27 NLT)

Why would God send Philip, one of the most significant leaders of the early church, away from where hundreds of lives were being impacted and to this desert road?

A man. *One* man.

It's incredible the lengths God will go to reach one person. There were crowds in Samaria, but one at a time is the Jesus way of changing the world.

I love that the angel tells Philip to leave his successful ministry to go down a road, without any explanation as to why, and the next verse begins, "So he started out."

Philip doesn't know why he's being asked to go, but he goes. He doesn't object to the direction. He doesn't even ask questions.

If *we* want to experience God's will for our lives, we need to listen for and be obedient to God's voice. If we follow, we'll walk into an amazing story God is writing and wants us to be a part of.

Philip doesn't know why he's being told to go, but he "started out, and he met the treasurer of Ethiopia, a eunuch of great authority" (Acts 8:27 NLT).

Because this man was an Ethiopian, and especially because he was a eunuch, Jewish people back then would have looked at him like God was *not* for him. They were wrong. God was for him, and he sent Philip to make sure this man knew it.

When Philip meets him, the eunuch is sitting in his chariot reading the book of Isaiah from the Old Testament. He's seeking God.

Then, "the Spirit told Philip, 'Go to that chariot and stay near it'" (v. 29). There's no way this guy could be influenced by Philip *unless* Philip was in close proximity with him.

And, just like Philip, if you follow God's leading, you're going to end up chasing some chariots.

The chariot you chase might be the gym where you work out. The grocery store where you shop. The café or restaurant where you're a regular. I think for sure it's your workplace and the neighborhood you live in.

God's going to put you in close proximity to people who are far from him and give you divine appointments to share Jesus. To get close to them, you won't be able to stay where you are.

That's what happened with Philip. Think about it: here was a man who spoke a different language but somewhere along the line must have learned Greek, who traveled a thousand miles by chariot, and who now was on a deserted road reading the Bible—and along came Philip. This wasn't a random occurrence; it was a God-given appointment.

What if you stopped assuming people in your proximity are there by accident? The person next to you on the plane, the server at your table in the restaurant, the stylist cutting your hair, the parent who sits next to you at your kid's game, the family who lives next door—what if you started considering them divine appointments God has known about since the beginning of time and has carefully orchestrated so your paths cross at just the right moment?

Philip "ran up to the chariot" (v. 30) and got to share Jesus. I *love* how Philip did it:

> He started with a question, drawn from the immediate situation.
> He listened.
> He shared the "good news about Jesus" (v. 35).

What we have to share with people is *good* news about *Jesus.* Philip didn't share his morals or his political views. He pointed to Jesus and got personal enough to invite the Ethiopian man to take a next step closer to God.

And the result?

> As they traveled along the road, they came to some water and the eunuch said, "Look, here is water. What can stand in the way of my being baptized?" And he gave orders to stop the chariot. Then both Philip and the eunuch went down into the water and Philip baptized him. (vv. 36–38)

Wow. What a story! And *God has stories like that planned for you.*

QUESTION: When you pray, "God, who is someone you want me to get close to, so they can get close to you?" who comes to mind?

CHALLENGE: Pray that God will give you a divine appointment in the next twenty-four hours, and then be ready for it to happen. Ask God to help you ask a question, listen, and then (if it feels right) share the Good News in a gracious way.

DAY 13

sent to invade earth

"FOR GOD SO LOVED THE WORLD that he gave his one and only Son."

Yes. You're aware. John 3:16. You know it. You've seen the guy holding up the sign at the football game. You've probably memorized the verse.

But have you really thought about it?

God sent Jesus from heaven to earth.

John said it this way, a couple chapters earlier: "The Word became flesh and made his dwelling among us" (1:14). I love how the Message translation describes it as "[Jesus] moved into the neighborhood."

Why? John said it's so we could see his glory, the glory of the Son who came from the Father.

Every year we remember it on December 25. We celebrate that Jesus came, and we call it Christmas. We do things like putting up trees, hanging lights on our houses, making cookies and fruitcakes, buying each other things we don't need, wearing ugly sweaters, and sending out cards that say, "Chillin' with My Gnomies." We call it Christmas but really . . . heaven was invading earth.

Jesus was sent, by God, in love (remember "For God so loved the world"), to invade earth with heaven—to love all the people God loves.

Jesus moved into our neighborhood and ambushed the world with God's love.

He loved all kinds of people. He loved people no one else would love. He loved people who were hard to love.

He loved in all kinds of ways. He loved with encouraging words and by meeting needs and by touching the untouchable. He loved by showing grace to people who were drowning in shame.

God sent Jesus to our neighborhood so that, through Jesus, God could love us up close.

And we could smile and say how great it is and maybe even join the weird guy at the football game by holding up a sign of our own. *Yeah, Jesus is sent by God to invade earth with heaven!*

Except that . . . *we* were sent by God to invade earth with heaven.

Everyone is familiar with John 3:16, but what about John 20:21? You know, the verse where Jesus said, "As the Father has sent me, I am sending you." Yep. That's right.

For God so loved the world that he gave *you*.

Oh. Gulp. That's . . . different.

So, God has sent us. What exactly are we supposed to do? Well, the Father is sending us as he sent Jesus. And he sent Jesus to our neighborhood so, through him, he could love people up close. Jesus gives us our mission: "A new command I give you: Love one another. As I have loved you, so you must love one another" (13:34).

God so loved the world he sent you to get close to people and love them the way Jesus loves.

That's pretty cool.

QUESTION: What if, instead of viewing your home, place of work, or school as your location by random chance, you assume it's the specific place God sent you? How would you think differently if you thought of the places you spend your time as your mission field?

CHALLENGE: How could you bring heaven to earth this week? What would be a way you could love "another" as Jesus loves you? Ask God and sit quietly listening until he gives you an idea. When he does, do it!

overcome the fear. take the risk.

A FEW YEARS AGO, I was speaking at a local state prison to a group of inmates. Afterward, a man came up to share his story. He was a big man who had clearly spent some time in the gym, and he had tattoos running up both arms and onto his neck.

He pulled a photograph out of his Bible. It was a picture of him as a younger man standing in his driveway. The picture was taken from the house, and you could see the street behind him. He said, "I lived at this place for seven years. Take a look at this and tell me what you notice about this picture."

The shot was taken on a summer day. His shirt had the sleeves cut off. He had a grease rag sticking out of his front pocket. He was holding a beer up toward the camera with one hand. I wasn't sure what I was looking for, but I noticed he was getting emotional. I desperately wanted to find what he wanted me to see.

Then I saw it. It was in the background, across the street, a little out of focus. I handed the picture back to him and said, "You lived across the street from a church." Then, without really thinking, I told him, "I'm sorry."

It wasn't my church. I wasn't the pastor there. I'd never set foot inside those doors. But I was sorry because I knew what his story was going to be. Sure enough, he had lived there for seven years, and not one time did someone from that church come over and knock on his door. The pastor never introduced himself. On some Sunday mornings he'd be in his driveway working on his motorcycle and would watch as people walked into the small neighborhood church in their Sunday suits and dresses. It's not that they didn't see him but rather were careful not to look at him or make eye contact. The only interaction he had with the church was an occasional note in his mailbox letting him know that his grass was too long and needed to be mowed.

After he told me his story, he asked, "Why didn't someone at least cross the street and tell me about Jesus? Maybe I wouldn't have come, but why didn't someone at least invite me? I don't understand. Why didn't at least one person walk across the street after church and just talk to me?"

He could only imagine how differently things would have gone if he had become a follower of Jesus at that time in his life. But in a drunken rage he'd killed another man and was spending decades in prison. He wanted to know, *"Why didn't someone just walk across the street?"*

At first I assumed his question was rhetorical, because the answer seemed so obvious to me. But he kept staring at me in silence, and I realized he didn't know. He wanted to understand. So I told him the truth. "You were so different from them. They were afraid." I think he suspected as much but just didn't want to believe it. He was angry but mostly sad, and he told me, "That's not okay."

He's right, of course, but I wasn't surprised. Not because I knew that particular church or its pastor. I wasn't surprised because I know *me*. And I'm not sure I would've made it across the street either.

There's something in us that wants to follow Jesus but doesn't want to cross the street. We want to do God's will as long as it doesn't lead us out of our comfort zones.

But to do what God wants requires proximity. Proximity can be risky. It was risky for Jesus to go into a graveyard to talk to a naked, bloody lunatic. It was risky for Philip to leave a revival and walk down a deserted road.

It'll feel risky for you to talk to your coworker about your faith, or start a spiritual conversation with your server, or invite your neighbor to church. But we all need to overcome the fear and take the risk.

QUESTION: Is there a person God has put in your life who scares you a little? It might be because this person is different from you, or because he or she is aggressive, or angry, or outspoken about beliefs or values you don't share. Who is that person for you?

CHALLENGE: Show that person—the one who scares you a little—the love of God. What's a specific way you can serve that person or meet a need they have or make their day a little better? You might be scared, but pray for courage—and do it!

present into presence

SOMETHING DRAMATIC HAPPENS when people get close to Jesus. All through the Gospels, we see that one action changed lives. The woman caught in adultery, the crazy man who lived in the graveyard, the blind guy on the side of the road, the prostitute who came bursting into the dinner party.

If people get in front of Jesus, in his presence—if they meet Jesus and experience the love of Jesus—they feel it, they respond to it, and they're changed by it. People need to get close to Jesus. And to get them there, we need to get close to them. When we do, dramatic things can happen.

We see this in Mark 2, where we meet four faith-filled guys who had a friend who was paralyzed. There was just no hope for this guy until, one day, hope came to the neighborhood.

Jesus showed up, and the four friends knew they had to get their buddy close to Jesus. So they went to his place, picked him up, and carried him to Jesus.

I love how it was a team effort. They did it together because the load was too heavy for just one to carry him alone. They could never get him to Jesus without working together. That can be true for us as well. If you're struggling to get someone in front of Jesus, you might want to have some other people help you. You could invite that person over for dinner along with some of your friends from church. Or start a fantasy football league or recurring group play date with that person and some of your faith-filled friends. Who knows what cool thing might happen?

In Mark 2, these four guys carried their friend to where Jesus was, but they still couldn't get him in front of Jesus. Jesus was inside a house, teaching, and the building was packed with people. So they did what any of us would do: "Since they could not get him to Jesus because of the crowd, they made an opening in the roof above Jesus by digging through it and then lowered the mat the man was lying on" (v. 4).

Okay, maybe we wouldn't do that, but these guys were willing to do whatever it took! We need to have that same can't-stop-won't-stop attitude about getting our friends to Jesus.

When the paralyzed man was lowered down into the room, Jesus forgave his sin *and* healed his legs. He did more than the friends expected. It was like a "buy one miracle get one free" special!

They got their friend close to Jesus, and it changed everything for him.

We need to be present with people so we can get them in the presence of Jesus. Because in the presence of Jesus there is power. In the presence of Jesus there is hope. In the presence of Jesus there is healing. In the presence of Jesus the impossible becomes possible.

And it's the presence of Jesus that will make all the difference for our friends, neighbors, coworkers, and family members.

You've probably heard that Kanye West put his faith in Jesus and gave his life and music to God. He put out a worship album called *Jesus Is King* and now has pastors present the gospel at his concerts.

How did it all happen?

An invitation.

Someone met Kanye at a grocery store and invited him to Placerita Bible Church in California. Kanye showed up. What are the chances? Well, apparently pretty good, if we just ask.

Kanye probably didn't realize it, but he was waiting for an invitation. And when he got one, he said yes and his life was changed.

I love it. It all happened because someone went up to Kanye at a grocery store, got close, and invited him to church. And getting him to church was important, because when believers meet together to worship, the presence of Jesus is there with them.

Who knows what could happen if you get close to someone and invite them? Who knows what they'd say? Who knows what it could lead to?

We need to be present with people so we can get them into the presence of Jesus.

QUESTION: Who has God put in your life who is far from him? What if that person is just waiting to be invited, even if they don't realize it?

CHALLENGE: Whoever that person is, make an invite. It might be an invitation to church, but if you feel that's not the best idea right now, you could invite the person out for coffee, or to your house for dinner, or whatever God leads you to do. Who knows what they'll say? And who knows what it could lead to?

WEEK 4

the practice of
doing
compassion

[the power of *and*]

real compassion acts

YEARS AGO, I picked up a book called *Body for Life*. For me, it was *Body for Three Months*. It's not that I stopped believing in the book. I do believe. In fact, at its beginning and end are dozens of before and after pictures of people who put the book into practice and experienced dramatic results.

Like all those people, I read the book. I took in all the information. I agreed with all of it. The difference is, they did what the book said while I just read it. I got information. They applied it.

That, however, was years ago. I am a better man today and live in an age of advanced technology. So about a year ago I downloaded an app called iFit. Why? Because I believe in the importance of health and exercise. So I put iFit on my phone. It has an amazing amount of great information. It tells me what I need to know to get in great shape. I love that it lists different body parts, and I can tap on each and learn what to do to increase strength in that area. Incredible information! And it's on my phone, so I have it with me all the time.

But I have to confess: I'm no healthier today than when I downloaded that app. Is the problem my belief? No, I do believe it's important. Is the problem the information on the app? No, it has all the right info. So, what's the problem? The problem is that I *feel* like I should get in better shape, but I am *not doing anything* to get in better shape.

In the Bible, we repeatedly see that Jesus felt compassion for people. I like that because I often feel compassion for people. Pretty cool, right? Jesus and I are so similar!

But there's a difference. When Jesus felt compassion, there was always an *and*. He felt compassion *and* he did something about it. Because of his compassion he touched the leper, fed the hungry, healed the blind man.

When I feel compassion, I often . . . just feel compassion. There is *not* always an *and*. I feel my throat clench up because of this poor person's plight. I shake my head in sadness. I may even shed a tear. But that's it. And, if I'm being honest, I feel kind of good about myself. Because other people may not have even noticed how that person was struggling. Other people may not have even cared. I did. I felt something.

But feeling something isn't enough. True compassion acts. There's always an *and*. If not, our compassion isn't really compassion. If not, James tells us, our faith is dead:

> What good is it, my brothers and sisters, if someone claims to have faith but has no deeds? Can such faith save them? Suppose a brother or a sister is without clothes and daily food. If one of you says to them, "Go in peace; keep warm and well fed," but does nothing about their physical needs, what good is it? In the same way, faith by itself, if it is not accompanied by action, is dead.
>
> But someone will say, "You have faith; I have deeds."
>
> Show me your faith without deeds, and I will show you my faith by my deeds. You believe that there is one God. Good! Even the demons believe that—and shudder. (James 2:14–19)

QUESTION: Why do you think it's so easy to feel compassion but not always so easy to do something about it?

CHALLENGE: Who is someone you have felt bad for but never done anything for? Find some way to "do" compassion for that person this week.

17

the *and*

SO MANY OF US CONFUSE our feelings for faith. We let ourselves off the hook because we feel the right way. We're kind of proud of how we feel. But the question is not, Did you feel anything? but, Did you do anything?

This hit home for me one night some years ago when I was up late flipping through the channels and came across a program showing children who were starving and had bloated stomachs. Most people would immediately have changed the channel, but I watched for a few moments and said a prayer for those kids.

Then I got up, thinking, *I'm glad I'm not the kind of person who just flips right through those channels. I'm glad I'm the kind of person who watches, who is filled with compassion, who prays.* Then, as I headed toward the refrigerator for my midnight snack, it hit me. That's not true faith and it's *not* compassion. Compassion isn't having pity on a child; it is sponsoring a child in faith.

Yesterday we read James 2:17, "Faith by itself, if it is not accompanied by action, is dead."

God wants us to know that it's not what we know but what we do with our knowledge that matters. Unfortunately, it's much easier to focus on what we know and to just want to know more.

We see this in some churchgoers who talk about the need for "deep teaching." Typically, they try to say it in an encouraging way. They come up to the pastor after the sermon and say, "I really enjoyed that message this morning. We need more deep teaching."

Umm. In other words, "Every other message you've ever preached *hasn't* been deep, but it's nice to know you're capable of one a year."

One time someone came up to me in the lobby after a service in which I preached a very practical sermon. The person said, "We really appreciated that message. The church we came from had more deep teaching. But we found your sermon to be helpful today." I didn't know what to say. *Thank you?*

I wonder sometimes if what this "deep teaching" crowd really wants is teaching they don't understand. They'd never say it that way. "Pastor, could you give us some teaching with big words we don't know? And if you could say it in a way that goes right over our heads, that would be perfect." That's not what they say—but I wonder if that's what they want.

Why? Because it's easier to *not* apply that kind of "deep teaching." I can nod my head in agreement, tell the preacher, "Good sermon" on the way out, and go on living the same way I have been. But God didn't give us the Bible for information. He gave it to us for transformation. It's not what we know but what we do with it that matters.

Feeling compassion isn't enough. Jesus didn't just feel compassion. There was always an *and*. When he met a leper, he felt compassion *and* did the one thing no one else would have done—he reached out and touched him.

We need to have an *and*.

We need an act of compassion to follow our feelings of compassion. There's something about feeling compassionate that makes you feel like you are compassionate, but no. That's not biblical compassion.

Real compassion doesn't just break your heart. It moves your muscles.

Feelings of compassion are God's call to action. The way you know whether you really choose compassion is not in how you feel but what you do.

Researchers at the University of British Columbia have done studies that demonstrate people who show support for their favorite causes on social media are *less* likely to donate money or volunteer their time.* They feel compassionate and, apparently, feel like that's compassion enough. It's not.

*Andrew Riley, "Slacktivism: 'Liking' on Facebook May Mean Less Giving," The University of British Columbia, November 8, 2013, https://news.ubc.ca/2013/11/08/slacktivism-liking-on-facebook-may-mean-less-giving/.

For instance, what did Jesus say we should do for people we are tempted to condemn? "Love your enemies and pray for those who persecute you" (Matt. 5:44). He didn't talk about feelings; he told us what we should *do*.

What if we have the right feelings but don't take action? Remember what James said: faith not accompanied by action is dead.

QUESTION: If I were to ask you, "Is your faith alive or dead?" what would you answer? Why would you give that answer? What would you point to as evidence for it?

CHALLENGE: Who is someone close to you who is hurting in some way? Perhaps this is even someone who lives in your house? What compassionate (and perhaps surprising) *action* could you take for that person?

who is it who's hurting?

I SOMETIMES WONDER how Jesus was able to show compassion so consistently. It's not so easy for me. I think the reason might be who Jesus saw.

Over the years I have taken my son on several skiing trips. We usually head to Colorado for three or four days to hit the slopes. We often see people wiping out and taking hard falls. Whenever we do, I feel a lot of compassion for them. (Full disclosure: my compassion may sometimes sound more like laughter.)

The last time we went skiing in Colorado, we got on the lift and headed toward the top of the mountain. My teenage son, already a much better skier than me, duly listened to my lecture about not going too fast and skiing within his limits.

When we finally got to the top, we were greeted by slopes with friendly sounding names like "Devil's Run," "Hell's Canyon," and my personal favorite, "Body Bag."

On one of our first runs, my son quickly disappeared out of sight while I skied from side to side, making my way safely and slowly. About halfway down the mountain, I noticed someone who had taken a hard fall. His skis and poles had flown in different directions. Immediately I felt sympathetic. *Poor guy, that's a rough way to start the day.* The skier was completely laid out, and I could hear him moaning. I hated it for him, but there wasn't much I could do. Then I realized, *That's my son!* I rushed over to him. He was hurt and in a lot of pain. We later found out he had snapped his clavicle.

My response in that moment is the difference between sympathy and compassion. I had feelings. That was sympathy. Then I did something about my feelings; that was Christlike, biblical compassion.

What's interesting to me is *why*. Why did I go from just feeling bad to doing something? When the wiped-out skier went from being some bro on the slopes to being my son, that changed everything. I assumed it was someone I didn't care about but realized it was actually someone I cared about deeply. That's what made me not just feel sorry but stop. When I realized it was my son, I was willing to do whatever was necessary to help him. Nothing and no one could stop me.

How was Jesus able to consistently show compassion? I think the reason might be who Jesus saw. He saw everyone as God's son or daughter. *Every* hurting person was a child of God.

Remember what Jesus called the woman who fought through the crowd to touch his garment for healing?

"Daughter" (Luke 8:48).

Of course he stopped. Of course he healed her.

And you know what? Every hurting person you see is a son or daughter of God.

QUESTION: What could help you to see a hurting person not as a stranger but as God's child and therefore someone you should care desperately about?

CHALLENGE: Think of a person you are disgruntled with for some reason. Ask God to help you see that person as his son or daughter who is deeply loved by him. Then, driven by that understanding, reach out to that person in love.

give me your heart

I WANT TO TEACH YOU a prayer that could transform how you treat people. You're going to love it, but there's a problem. You have to pray this prayer with your eyes open.

I grew up believing there were right times to pray, such as before meals and at bedtime. Praying at church was also a thing. Heaving up a desperate Hail Mary prayer before a test you didn't study for was also deemed appropriate.

However, in the Bible we are encouraged to "pray continually" (1 Thess. 5:17) and to "pray . . . on all occasions . . . and always keep on praying" (Eph. 6:18).

Turns out there is a right time to pray, and it is *now*.

Not only was I taught that there was a right time to pray but also that there was a right way to pray: head bowed and eyes closed.

In fact, in our family, if your head wasn't bowed and your eyes weren't closed during prayer, it was considered a serious infraction. When the dinnertime prayer was over, my little sister would start calling out the perps. It was intense!

She was like, "I'm Chris Hansen from NBC. Why don't you have a seat?" The cameras would come out, and they would rewind the tape and show when my eyes were open.

I'd protest, "It was just for a split second!" and add my tried-and-true counterattack: "How do you know my eyes were open if your eyes were closed?"

At the time, that was the best argument I could come up with, but I can now make a stronger case. If we are supposed to pray "all the time," then we're going to have to pray with our eyes open. In fact, learning to pray with my eyes open has changed my relationship with God and the way I see people.

I've come to believe that to love people one at a time like Jesus did, I *have to* practice eyes-open prayer.

What exactly should we pray? I don't believe there's one right prayer, but I have found one to be especially powerful. Are you ready for it?

Jesus, give me your heart for this person.

We ask God to give us his heart for each person he puts in our path. Your lazy husband or frustrating wife, your teenager who won't do what you ask, the homeless person blocking the street corner, the server who gets sarcastic with you for no reason.

Jesus, give me your heart for this person.

In his book *Unshockable Love*, pastor John Burke asks people to imagine finding a Rembrandt painting covered in mud. You wouldn't focus on the mud or treat it like mud. Your primary concern wouldn't be the mud, though it would need to be removed. You would just be amazed to have something so valuable in your care.

Having Jesus's heart for people allows us to see the masterpiece behind the mud and desire to have the mud removed so the masterpiece can be revealed.

Praying, eyes open, "Jesus, give me your heart for this person" helps us to see what Jesus saw, feel what Jesus felt, and do what Jesus did.

QUESTION: When you look at people, do you tend to see the mud (the character flaws and frustrating personality traits) or the masterpiece (the amazing person God created them to be)?

CHALLENGE: Today, with each person God puts in your path, pray, "Jesus, give me your heart for this person."

20

i was wrong

ONE OF MY FAVORITE PREACHERS is the late Fred Craddock. Though he was a pastor, his father wasn't a believer. In fact, his dad was skeptical about Christianity and extremely cynical about the church. Fred tried and tried to get his dad to come. But every time he was invited to church, his dad would say, "I know what you want—another name and another pledge. You don't care about me. You just want another name and another dollar."

You know people like that. God calls us to love one at a time, to get close to people so they can get close to Jesus, but some people aren't very open. Some people may even be outright antagonistic toward you, especially about your faith.

What do you do with a person like that?

Bless those who persecute you; bless and do not curse. Rejoice with those who rejoice; mourn with those who mourn. Live in harmony with one another. Do not be proud, but be willing to associate with people of low position. Do not be conceited.

Do not repay anyone evil for evil. Be careful to do what is right in the eyes of everyone. If it is possible, as far as it depends on you, live at peace with everyone. Do not take revenge, my dear friends, but leave room for God's wrath, for it is written: "It is mine to avenge; I will repay," says the Lord. On the contrary:

> "If your enemy is hungry, feed him;
>   if he is thirsty, give him something to drink.
> In doing this, you will heap burning coals on his
>   head."

Do not be overcome by evil, but overcome evil with good. (Rom. 12:14–21)

Did you notice?

Nowhere in that passage does it tell us how to feel. Should we feel compassion for someone whose heart is hardened toward God? Yes, absolutely.

But feeling compassion won't overcome their unbelief. Compassionate *action* might. So, if he's hungry, feed him. If she's thirsty, give her a drink.

Fred Craddock's father got cancer and had to have his throat removed. He was in the hospital for a long time and wasted away to seventy-four pounds. Even though he'd always rejected his son's church, people from the church came to visit him and brought food and flowers and cards.

One time Fred was sitting with his father, reading him the cards and notes from the church people. His dad grabbed a pen and paper and wrote words from Shakespeare's *Hamlet*: "In this harsh world, draw your breath in pain to tell my story."

Craddock asked, "What is your story, Dad?"

His father wrote, "I was wrong. I was wrong."*

QUESTION: What is your typical reaction to someone who rejects God and is antagonistic toward faith? Do you have God's heart for this person whom he loves and wants to come to him in faith?

CHALLENGE: Who in your life has been difficult about your faith? What could you do to "bless those who persecute you; bless and do not curse" (v. 14)? Compassionate action might start to overcome their unbelief, so go do it.

*John Blake, "A Preaching 'Genius' Faces His Toughest Convert," CNN, December 14, 2011, https://www.cnn.com/2011/11/27/us/craddock-profile /index.html.

WEEK 5

the practice of
salting

[extra mile mentality]

God's dream for your life

JESUS'S MOST FAMOUS SERMON is called "The Sermon on the Mount," but it could be titled "God's Dream for Your Life."

Jesus taught people God's plan for them. We've been looking at examples of how Jesus impacted one person at a time, but in his Sermon on the Mount, he gave some core teachings that laid the foundation for one at a time living. Specifically, Jesus raised the bar on how we are to treat others.

Jesus reframed how we're to look at and treat people who are difficult to love. Six times he brought up what people had previously been taught by saying, "You have heard that it was said." That was a common rabbinical phrase typically used when a rabbi was going to reference a teaching from the Old Testament law, called the

Torah. Jesus was pointing out a commonly understood and widely accepted teaching from Scripture. It would be like me saying, "I know you were taught in school," or "I know your parents said," or "The church you grew up in believed . . ."

Jesus would begin, "You have heard that it was said," and everyone would nod at his quote—then he would surprise them with his next word, "but." *But? What? You can't* but *what's been said.*

He would then continue, "But I tell you," and introduce a new standard of how we were to relate to others. He wasn't contradicting the law; he was clarifying it and giving a deeper understanding of what God was really after when the law was given.

I want to walk through a few of Jesus's Sermon on the Mount teachings to help us better understand the one at a time life. I need to warn you that some of what Jesus taught will be hard to receive. It contradicts the way most of us think. You may even feel defensive at times. You will think of a person or situation in your life and begin to rationalize and justify why you're not following his teaching. If you decide to live this way, it may feel unnatural and uncomfortable at first. But Jesus has made it clear that if you align your life and relationships with his way of treating people, two things will happen.

First, you will be blessed. The Sermon on the Mount starts with a series of statements that begin with this promise, "Blessed are those who . . ." Everyone I know wants to live a blessed and happy life, but Jesus taught that the path that actually leads there will often feel like it's taking you in the opposite direction. What Jesus teaches may seem counterintuitive, but if you choose it, you will be blessed.

Second, you will make a difference. Everyone I know wants to be blessed *and* wants to make a difference in this world. In Matthew 5 Jesus told his followers, "You are the salt of the earth . . . [and] the light of the world" (vv. 13–14). Then he laid out how to treat people in a way that shines a light and adds salt.

In those days, salt served several purposes. It was used to preserve food, which we don't do as much anymore. It was also used, as is still common today, to add flavor. I think we can all agree that some things are not good without salt, like a baked potato or corn on the cob. No offense, but if you eat corn on the cob without salt, I don't trust you. You've got to salt your cob! If you're on a date with someone who orders corn on the cob, that's a red flag, but if they don't salt it, just get up and leave.

If we treat people the way Jesus teaches, it adds salt. When we *don't* treat people this way, it's like corn on the cob without salt—no one is interested. If we apply his one at a time approach to the people in our lives, Jesus said it will make God look good, and people will notice and get an appetite for God (v. 16).

QUESTION: What do you assume is the path to living a blessed life that makes a difference in the world? How does it compare to what Jesus taught in the Sermon on the Mount?

CHALLENGE: Read the Sermon on the Mount (Matthew 5–7). Ask God to show you what specifically you most need to apply to your life right now.

second mile living

WHAT'S YOUR DEFAULT SETTING when it comes to dealing with difficult people? The bully at school. The rude coworker. The steamrolling sibling. The annoying neighbor. The ungrateful child. The selfish friend. How do you respond when someone hurts you? Betrays you? Rejects you? Ridicules you? Takes advantage of you? Gossips about you?

Let's take a quick walk through some of Jesus's teaching in the Sermon on the Mount and see how he wants us to respond.

He said, "You have heard that it was said, 'Eye for eye, and tooth for tooth'" (Matt. 5:38). Not only have I heard that, I like it. Hit me, and I hit you back. Honk at me, and I will honk back every time, bro!

Jesus was referencing an Old Testament law that made sure a punishment or retribution didn't exceed the initiating offense. He said, "You have heard" but then gave a new standard: "But I tell you, do not resist an evil person" (v. 39).

Oh. That's . . . different.

Jesus then took this broad statement and gave specific examples. Warning: this is where it gets uncomfortable.

Scenario #1: "If anyone slaps you on the right cheek, turn to them the other cheek also" (v. 39). Seriously? I don't get to hit back? Instead, I'm supposed to say, "Thank you. Might I have another?" Yes. Jesus said if someone disrespects you, don't resist them; turn to them your other cheek also. You won't feel like it. But if you do this, it will bless your life and impact others. People will notice, and it will make God look good.

Scenario #2: "And if anyone wants to sue you and take your shirt, hand over your coat as well" (v. 40). In those days, people might have several shirts but typically only *one* coat. When it was cold at night, that coat became their blanket. Exodus 22 essentially ensured everyone had a right to a coat since it was needed for protection from the elements. Because having a coat was considered a basic human right, suing someone for their coat wasn't permitted. But sometimes following Jesus means letting go of our rights. Sometimes letting go of our rights is the righteous thing to do.

Scenario #3: "If anyone forces you to go one mile, go with them two miles" (v. 41). The problem I have with this is "forces." If someone *asks* me to go one mile, I may not feel like it, but I probably still need to get my steps in, so I'll go a mile if asked. But *forced*? No, thanks.

There was a law back then that a Roman soldier could force civilians into acts of service, but there were limitations. A Roman soldier could make a Jew carry his pack for one mile, but not any farther. The Jewish person had to carry the hated Roman soldier's pack a mile but couldn't be forced to go a second mile.

Yet here was Jesus telling the Jews of his day not to fight against Roman oppression but to actually do *more* than asked. Can you imagine if, at the end of the first mile, a God-worshiping Jewish man said to a Roman soldier, "You know what? I don't mind going a second mile if that would help you out"?

It would feel like he's giving up power, but if you think about it, isn't he taking some control back? No one is making him do it; he's *choosing* it. He might have come home a little later than he had planned, but he walks in the door with dignity.

My guess is the Roman soldier wouldn't have known what to say. I'm sure he'd tell the other soldiers about it. "You wouldn't believe what happened to me today. I made a Jewish guy carry my pack one mile, and he voluntarily carried it two." People would notice.

QUESTION: Jesus teaches his followers to have a second mile mentality with one person at a time, even when that person is an enemy who is making our lives miserable. What would it look like for you to live that way today?

CHALLENGE: The next time someone insults you, say something nice to them. If your spouse criticizes you, compliment them. If someone blames you, bless them. If your server is short with you, give a more generous tip than you would normally give. If your boss is especially demanding, pray for them and drop them a note of encouragement. Go the second mile. It'll bless your life, and you'll make a difference in the world as you make God look good.

who lives this way?

MAYBE WHEN YOU READ Jesus's teaching in the Sermon on the Mount, you think, *Who does that? Who gets hit and turns the other cheek? Who gets sued and hands over their coat? Who gets forced to go one mile and then volunteers a second? I can see why it would make a difference, but who actually lives that way?*

Jesus.

He was *always* doing this. Philippians 2 says when we consider others better than ourselves and put their needs ahead of our own, we're following the example of Jesus, who made himself nothing and took on the nature of a servant.

Then, at the end of his earthly life, Jesus, the Son of God, was falsely accused. He was unjustly arrested. He was violently beaten. A soldier blindfolded him. Others slapped him and spat in his face. He was brutally mocked. One of the soldiers said, "Prophesy to us, Messiah. Who hit you?" (Matt. 26:68). The irony, of course, is that Jesus knew. He knew each soldier's name. He knew the number of hairs on each soldier's head. Jesus got slapped but he didn't slap back. He could have.

Don't mistake his love for weakness. There may have been a garrison of soldiers abusing him that day, but in Matthew 26 Jesus made it clear that, if he wanted, he could command twelve legions of angels to come to his defense. If you're a little rusty on your first-century math, that adds up to 72,000 angels. All Jesus had to do was say the word. With every insult hurled, with every punch thrown, with every crack of the whip, with every cry of agony, with every drop of blood shed, 72,000 angels grew more restless. All he had to do was say the word and it would all be over.

But Jesus didn't need the angels' help. With only a blink of his eyes, he could have struck the soldiers blind. A nod of his head had the power to leave them paralyzed. One word from his mouth could curse every last one of them to hell.

Finally, after he was nailed to the cross, he spoke for the first time. All of heaven's armies leaned forward, ready for him to give the command. What did he say? "Father, forgive them" (Luke 23:34). He prayed that God would forgive his enemies.

It's hard to think of it this way, but when you're mistreated and taken advantage of, it provides you an opportunity to love and live like Jesus. We'd prefer to change the world one social media post at a time, but it's more likely your greatest impact will come one offense at a time, one insult at a time, one irritation at a time, one aggravation at a time, one extra mile at a time.

QUESTION: Who is an "enemy" who has caused you a lot of pain?

CHALLENGE: Jesus tells us to bless our enemies and forgive those who have hurt us. It's time to forgive that person. If that doesn't feel possible right now, what steps will you take to journey toward giving forgiveness?

24

who lives this way . . . other than Jesus?

IN THE LAST CHAPTER, I acknowledged that you might be asking, about Jesus's Sermon on the Mount, *Who does that? Who actually lives that way?* And I gave you an answer.

Jesus.

Perhaps your response to that was, *Okay. Good point. But, well, who else does that? Like, does anyone other than Jesus actually live that way?*

Meet Julio.

Julio Diaz—a social worker in his early thirties—often got off the subway one stop before his station in the Bronx so he could eat at his favorite diner. One night he stepped off the No. 6 train and began walking toward the exit when an intimidating teenager approached, flashed a knife, and demanded all his money. Diaz pulled out his wallet, handed it over, and said, "Here you go."

Let's pause the story. I wonder what you would do after handing over your wallet. Hurry away? Feel victimized? Tell the police? Post on Facebook about how awful the world has become?

Un-pause.

Diaz handed over his wallet and said, "Here you go." The teenager took it and began walking away, but Diaz called after him. "Hey, wait a minute. You forgot something."

Diaz told him, "If you're going to be robbing people for the rest of the night, you might as well take my coat to keep you warm."

Diaz began taking off his coat. The boy was confused. "Why are you doing this?" he demanded.

"If you're willing to risk your freedom for a few dollars," Diaz responded, "then I guess you must really need the money."*

Let's pause the story again. If you got mugged every night for a year, would it ever even occur to you to give the mugger your coat?

My guess is it wouldn't. Me neither.

---

* "A Victim Treats His Mugger Right," *NPR Morning Edition*, March 28, 2008, http://www.npr.org/templates/story/story.php?storyId=89164759 &sc=emaf.

Unless . . . we read the Sermon on the Mount and take Jesus seriously when he said the whole thing about "handing over your coat as well."

But was he serious? Did he mean it literally? Are we really supposed to live this way?

Yes.

If we really want to be Jesus's followers, we are. And we *will*, if we want to impact people with God's love, one at a time.

Un-pause. Remember, Julio Diaz was just robbed at knifepoint by a teenager. As the boy walked away, Diaz called him back and offered him his coat. The boy asked, "Why are you doing this?" Diaz told the boy he must really need the money.

Then he continued, "I mean, all I wanted to do was get dinner, and if you really want to join me . . . hey, you're more than welcome."

This teenager stared at Diaz. I'm sure he was thinking, *Are you serious? Who is this guy? Is this real life?* And then . . . he agreed to go out to eat with him!

Why? I don't know, but my guess is that he was drawn by love. Everyone is attracted to love.

So the mugger and the muggee (pretty sure *muggee* is not a word; I just made that up) head off together to Diaz's favorite diner. While they eat, the manager, dish-washers, and wait staff come over to say hi to Diaz. Turns out, Diaz was everyone's favorite customer. (And had just become the mugger's favorite muggee. Yes, I'm sticking with my new word.)

"You know everybody here," the teenager said. "Do you own this place?"

"No." Diaz smiled. "I just eat here a lot."

"But you're even nice to the dishwasher."

"Well," Diaz responded, "haven't you been taught you should be nice to everybody?"

"Yeah, but I didn't think people actually behaved that way."

Diaz asked the young man what he wanted out of life but got only a sad, blank look in response.

Finally, the bill arrived. Diaz told the teenager, "Look, I guess you're going to have to pay for this, because you have my money and I can't pay. So, if you give me my wallet back, I'll gladly treat you."

The teen didn't even think about it. He immediately returned Diaz's wallet. Diaz paid for the meal and gave the boy twenty dollars. But he asked for something in return—the knife—which the teenager handed over.

Wow

You or I probably would've given the robber our wallet, rushed home, and spent the rest of our lives complaining about how bad people are. Diaz saw an opportunity to love someone who needed some love and helped turn a bad person into someone at least a little bit better.

How do we have Christlike influence?

How do we change the world?

One at a time.

Often by going the second mile.

QUESTION: Think of a time you were wronged. How did you respond? What was the result of your response? How might it have been different if you "salted" your response by living out Jesus's Sermon on the Mount?

CHALLENGE: Decide that the next time you are wronged—it might be today by a coworker or another driver on the road—your response will be guided by Jesus's teaching in the Sermon on the Mount.

what happens when we live this way?

I KNOW WHAT YOU may be thinking. I just might be thinking it too.

But . . . if I live this way, I'm going to suffer. I mean, Jesus is asking me to let people hurt me. And I may be taken advantage of.

Yes, that could be true.

Do you know what it would mean? It would mean you'd really know and become like Jesus. Because Jesus let people hurt him. Jesus allowed people to take advantage of him. Jesus suffered.

And if we want to know him and be like him, we need to suffer as well.

Paul talked about how there's nothing greater than knowing and becoming like Jesus:

> What is more, I consider everything a loss because of the surpassing worth of knowing Christ Jesus my Lord, for whose sake I have lost all things. I consider them garbage, that I may gain Christ and be found in him, not having a righteousness of my own that comes from the law, but that which is through faith in Christ—the righteousness that comes from God on the basis of faith. I want to know Christ—yes, to know the power of his resurrection and participation in his sufferings, becoming like him in his death, and so, somehow, attaining to the resurrection from the dead. (Phil. 3:8–11)

Notice that Paul said he *wanted* to participate in Jesus's sufferings. Why? Because if you think knowing and being like Jesus is the best life has to offer, and Jesus suffered for doing good and loving people, then you want to suffer for doing good and loving people.

I read a book a few years ago called *Chasing Francis*. It's a story about a megachurch pastor named Chase who is feeling burned out. He thinks he might be done with ministry. As things unravel, the elders of his church tell him he needs to take some time away.

He ends up going to Italy, and while there joins some Franciscan friars on a spiritual pilgrimage where they retrace the life of Saint Francis of Assisi.

Toward the end of the journey, they visit a community home for men dying of AIDS. Chase feels incredibly apprehensive. A nun serving there explains that most of the men there have no one to take care of them. They have been disowned and abandoned. She tells them, "You've come just in time. We need to give the men baths."

Chase scrambles for a reason he couldn't possibly help but isn't quick enough. He is soon standing before a man who is six feet tall and weighs less than one hundred pounds. This man is lying in a bathtub, naked and frail. The nurse begins to wash him as Chase looks on, relieved that his help isn't necessary.

But then, Chase says,

> She handed me a rag. "Would you mind washing his genitals?" she asked evenly. I was speechless. The stickman looked up at me for the first time as if to say, "What will you choose to do now?" I pushed back against my revulsion and plunged the sponge beneath the water. As I began to wash him my terror and embarrassment was replaced by peace.*

When he is finished, they go back downstairs, where Chase is met by one of his Franciscan friends. The friend notices that Chase looks different, like somehow his load has been lightened. The friar asks, "What happened up

*Ian Morgan Cron, *Chasing Francis: A Pilgrim's Tale* (Colorado Springs: NavPress, 2006).

what happens when we live this way?

there?" Chase pauses for a moment, then replies, "I think I became a Christian."

QUESTION: When you read Paul saying that he wanted to suffer for Jesus so he could better know Jesus and become more like him, how does it strike you? Are you that passionate about knowing and becoming like Jesus?

CHALLENGE: What's something you could do to "suffer" for Jesus? It might be something that would force you to swallow your pride, like apologizing to someone, or something that seems gross or beneath you, like bathing a sick person. Pray for help in thinking of how you could suffer for Jesus and then do it, prayerfully, asking God to use that experience to help you know and become more like Jesus.

WEEK 6

the practice of
giving grace

[don't be a prig]

lead with love

HAVE YOU EVER BEEN to a Cheesecake Factory? If so, you've seen the menu. Have you tried to *lift it*? It weighs just a little more than a bowling ball. The list of what they offer goes on and on and on. You can order shepherd's pie or four-cheese pasta or a French dip cheeseburger or chicken potstickers or Buffalo wings or almond crusted salmon salad or Korean fried cauliflower or pepperoni flatbread pizza or fish tacos or chicken Bellagio or taquitos or crab and artichoke dip or Cajun jambalaya pasta or . . . more than 240 other options! Literally.

What can't you get at Cheesecake Factory? A hot dog I checked. That's it. Everything else is there.

You're sitting at the table, reading through the menu, when the server comes up and asks you, "Have you decided?"

"No, I'm only on page 27," you reply. "I'll let you know when I get to chapter 8."

Finally you make your choice. You get it. You eat it. Then the server asks, "Did you leave room for cheesecake?" Well, of course you didn't leave room for cheesecake. You don't think you can do it. But you have to. I mean, it is the *Cheesecake* Factory. So you say, "Sure, I'll take a piece of cheesecake." The server responds, "That's great! Which kind?" You get a little nervous. "Which kind?"

"Yes," the server explains. "You have thirty-four choices."

For real! They offer thirty-four different kinds of cheesecake!

Do you know the Bible says Jesus offers two things? Yep. "We have seen his glory, the glory of the one and only Son, who came from the Father, full of grace and truth" (John 1:14).

Grace and truth.

Yes, I understand we could come up with a long, Cheesecake Factory menu–size list of all the things we receive from Jesus: blessing, salvation, sanctification, courage, healing, wisdom. But I wonder if, in some sense, it all fits within grace and truth.

Regardless, I think it can be helpful to consider that what we have to offer, as Jesus's followers, are grace and truth. With every person we meet, our hope is that they experience God's grace and embrace God's truth for their lives.

It might help make this a bit more practical (and will set up some memorable alliteration in a moment) if we use the word *love* instead of *grace*. We're told in Ephesians 4:15 to "[speak] the truth in love." That's what we have to offer: love and truth.

God puts people in our lives so that, through us, they can feel God's love for them and hear God's truth for them.

Sounds great. Here's the problem: we lead with truth.

Why is that an issue?

Well, it intimidates people. They're not wanting someone to come at them with truth. You know who else doesn't want someone coming at them with truth? *You.* You didn't wake up this morning hoping someone would share truth that would prove you're wrong about something important. That's intimidating. And that's why non-Christians aren't excited to hear from Christians.

Leading with truth intimidates the people who need to hear that truth, and it intimidates *you*. Most Christians aren't excited to share Jesus with non-Christians because they think of it as telling people they're wrong and trying to convince them of our truth. (And we're not effective, because most people don't want to be convinced of anything.)

But—good news—we aren't afraid of loving people. Right? And most people want to be loved.

See, the problem is that we lead with truth when we need to be leading with love. ("Lead with love" is the memorable alliteration I promised.)

Jesus led with love. With the woman caught in adultery, he ended with truth, "Go now and leave your life of sin" (John 8:11), but he led with love. We see it all the time. When Jesus met someone far from God, someone caught in sin, he always led with love.

Don't you think that's why sinful people wanted to be around him? Jesus was the only sinless person to ever walk the earth, yet the most sinful people wanted to be around him. Why? I think it's because Jesus didn't make them feel worse. He made them feel loved.

Jesus knew a secret that Christians today have lost: it's love that turns a life around. The way to change lives isn't by judging people but by embracing them. Not by pointing out their sins but by pointing the way to hope.

People need truth and love, but we need to follow Jesus's example and lead with love. Because it's love that builds a relationship, love that opens a person's ears to hear, love that opens hearts to the Good News, and love that leads people to repentance.

Love leads people to repent? Yep. That's what the Bible teaches. Titus 2:11–12 says, "For the grace of God has appeared that offers salvation to all people. It teaches us to say 'No' to ungodliness and worldly passions, and to live self-controlled, upright and godly lives in this present age." The offer of God's grace, not the threat of his wrath, leads people to salvation and repentance.

That's why Jesus led with love. And if we want to follow Jesus in having a one at a time impact on people, we will lead with love too.

QUESTION: How might it change the thinking of non-Christians if they defined *evangelism* as "mostly being loved by Christians"? How would it change your thinking about evangelism if your approach was to lead with love rather than truth?

CHALLENGE: Think of a person who doesn't believe in Jesus. At some point you'll want to share truth with them—the truth of their sin, who Jesus is, and their need for him to save them—but what if you led with love? Come up with some ideas to love the person in practical, big, significant ways. Then . . . get started!

DAY 27

tempted to condemn

CAN I ASK a kind of awkward personal question? Who are you tempted to condemn?

Your mother?

Your annoying coworker?

The spouse who cheated on you?

The child who broke your heart?

Those "friends" on Facebook who are always bragging about their perfect lives?

The contractor who swindled you?

The business partner who lied to you?

The relative who made you feel unimportant growing up?

Your boss?

Your employee?

The person at church who seems like such a hypocrite?

Those Democrats?

Those Republicans?

The neighbor with the dog that won't stop barking?

Who are you tempted to write off? To blame for your hurt? To shame for their sin? If there was someone or some group you could grab, bring to God, and accuse, who would it be? Who is the person—like the woman caught in adultery whom the religious leaders dragged before Jesus in John 8—you wouldn't mind throwing stones at?

Sometimes self-righteous anger comes not from something done to you but something you've done. I think of the national Christian leader some years ago who fought intensely against gay rights and the legalization of gay marriage— and then it came out that he was engaged in sexual relationships with young men in his church and male prostitutes. That's an especially scandalous example.

Here's one that's more common. Am I crazy, or are the people who get the angriest at "bad drivers" actually bad drivers themselves? Psychologists talk about *projection*, a subconscious defense mechanism people use in which they project their issues onto others in order to cope with their own guilty feelings. So that person you wouldn't mind making the target of your stone throwing—is it possible the anger you feel toward them comes from some negative feelings you have about yourself?

More often, our anger is the result of something done to us. When we hold on to bitterness and anger toward a person, it has a way of leaking out and infecting our other relationships. The term for this is *transference*. Our resentment toward a parent can cause us to have misplaced anger toward our spouse. Fury that we feel toward a coworker has a way of following us home and transferring over to our kids. Anger is a cancer that spreads.

Is it possible the anger you feel toward someone is more about someone else who has hurt you than about that person?

QUESTION: Who are you tempted to condemn?

CHALLENGE: Read Psalm 139:23–24.

> Search me, God, and know my heart;
>   test me and know my anxious thoughts.
> See if there is any offensive way in me,
>   and lead me in the way everlasting.

Pray, asking God to reveal to you the true reason you're tempted to condemn this person and to lead you in the way of Jesus—to recognize your own sin and drop your stones.

DAY 28

does condemning work?

QUESTION: HAS CONDEMNING a person ever changed a person?

Seriously. Have you ever met someone who told you, "Well, I was always this certain way, but then I met this hate-filled person who made me feel condemned, and that's when my whole life changed!"

No, you haven't. Neither have I.

Another question: Has feeling condemned ever helped *you* to change? Has condemnation ever led you to transformation? I bet not, because that's not the way it works. It's not condemnation but kindness that leads us to repentance (see Rom. 2:4).

Angrily pointing out people's sins doesn't lead them out of those sins. Don't confuse your bitterness and hatred with showing tough love. Loathing doesn't lead to life change.

In the Sermon on the Mount, Jesus talked about how we're to treat others, and he warned against the seriousness of anger. Jesus did something rather shocking—he put people with anger in their hearts in the same circle as murderers. In Matthew 5:21, Jesus said, "You have heard that it was said to the people long ago, 'You shall not murder, and anyone who murders will be subject to judgment.'"

People then and now would look at that and say, "Well, I would never murder anyone." In fact, people sometimes defend their wrongdoing by saying, "It's not like I killed anybody."

Everyone agrees with the command, "Thou shall not murder." (If you come across someone who does disagree, my suggestion is to run away. Don't get into a debate with someone who takes the stance that "murder is always an option.") We are not okay with murder—but check out how Jesus expanded the circle: "But I tell you that anyone who is angry with a brother or sister will be subject to judgment" (v. 22).

Jesus was saying that if you have anger in your heart, you can't compare yourself to a murderer and feel good about yourself. I have never murdered anyone, but there have been many times when I've become angry and expressed my anger in hurtful ways: raising my voice, calling names, showing disrespect, or gossiping about the person. Our tendency is to dismiss all that as no big deal. Everyone gets a little carried away now and then. But Jesus said, "No, it *is* a big deal."

You might feel good because when you get angry you don't yell or call names. You're not the type to pick up a rock and throw it at someone. But instead you withdraw; you go silent. Not to collect yourself but to hurt the other person. You know full well your ongoing silence and passive-aggressive spirit are driven by anger.

One of my friends, when he starts to get angry, will say, "Here's the thing . . ." Then he's going to look at you with a smile—but make no mistake, it's an angry smile. He murders with a smile on his face. Another friend of mine will say, whenever she's angry, "I just find it funny . . ." If she starts a sentence that way, just know what she's about to say is *not* something she found funny, and you'd better not laugh.*

The religious leaders were angry and full of self-righteous hatred as they dragged the woman caught in adultery before Jesus. As the story unfolds, we get to see the contrast between the condemning way of the religious leaders and the compassionate, one at a time way of Jesus.

The religious leaders were holding stones, waiting for Jesus to grant permission for them to condemn, but when Jesus spoke, he said, "Let any one of you who is without sin be the first to throw a stone at her" (John 8:7).

One by one, the religious leaders—who were guilty of sin—dropped their stones.

*And by "friend" I mean "wife." When she reads this footnote, she will say, "I just find it funny . . ."

Then the only one left was Jesus—who wasn't guilty of sin. Jesus *could have* condemned her, but he looked at her with eyes full of compassion and said, "Then neither do I condemn you. . . . Go now and leave your life of sin" (v. 11).

That's how you change a life. Not by condemning but through compassion. Kindness leads to repentance.

QUESTION: Think of all the people you've ever judged, gotten angry with, or condemned. What did you want to change about those people? What impact did your condemnation have on them?

CHALLENGE: Think of a person you currently want to judge, be angry with, or condemn. What do you want to change about that person? How could you—now understanding that, as a sinner, you have no right to judge and that it's kindness that leads people to repentance—show that person the kind of compassion Jesus showed the woman caught in adultery? *That's* your challenge. Find a way to show kindness to the person at whom you want to throw stones.

the key to everything

I ONCE MET A MAN named Adam.

I want to tell you about Adam, but before I do, I want to ask you to read Titus 2:11–14.

> For the grace of God has appeared that offers salvation to all people. It teaches us to say "No" to ungodliness and worldly passions, and to live self-controlled, upright and godly lives in this present age, while we wait for the blessed hope—the appearing of the glory of our great God and Savior, Jesus Christ, who gave himself for us to redeem us from all wickedness and to purify for himself a people that are his very own, eager to do what is good.

We're told it's the grace of God that offers salvation. You probably already knew that. But did you notice that it's also God's *grace* (not fear of God's wrath) that teaches people to say no to ungodliness and leads them to want to live good lives for Jesus? Did you know that?

It seems grace is the key to everything.

So . . . Adam.

He told me he had been incarcerated and that he was illiterate when he went to prison. But another inmate, who was a follower of Jesus, realized Adam was illiterate. He told Adam he would teach him to read and write, using the Gospel of Mark.

By the time he was released, Adam had not only learned to read about Jesus but had become a follower of Jesus. When he got out, he began attending a small church in a small town. I don't know what crime put Adam in prison, but somehow people in the church found out. Some were upset that he was now at their church.

One longtime, prominent family told the pastor, "Hey, look. You either need to ask Adam to leave, or we're going to leave." The pastor explained that Adam was welcome at their church. That family left. It began to look like other families were going to follow them.

Adam told me he started thinking it might be best for him to leave. He didn't want to create division or make a bigger mess for the pastor to have to clean up. Then, one Sunday after the sermon, the pastor stood before the congregation and asked Adam to come up to the front. Adam knew what was about to happen. The pastor must have found out about his crimes. He was going to tell everyone and ask Adam to leave.

Adam made his way to the front with his head down, ashamed of what he had done and embarrassed for what was about to happen. When he was standing with the pastor, the pastor announced, "I want everyone to know I've made an important decision. Since Adam has been released from prison, he's had a hard time finding work, so I want to offer him a job helping take care of our church facilities."

The pastor reached into his pocket and pulled out an extra set of keys to the church. He gave them to Adam and said, "You're going to be needing these to open and close the church on Sundays."

Tears ran down Adam's cheeks as he told me this story. He paused, collecting himself, then said, "It was the first time in my life I'd ever had a key to anything."

For the first time, he felt truly loved and accepted.

Oh—I should've mentioned where I met Adam. I was speaking not at a prison but at a pastor's conference. Why did I meet Adam there? Because he has been a pastor at that church for the past six years.

That's what happens when people—one at a time— experience the love and grace of Jesus through his followers.

QUESTION: In what ways has experiencing the amazing(ly outrageous) grace of God changed *your* life?

the key to everything

CHALLENGE: Sometimes when something becomes familiar, we can lose the wonder of it. That can happen with grace. Take some time—now if you have it, as soon as possible if not—to sit in God's presence and ask him to restore your amazement that he loves you unconditionally and perfectly. Commit to not leaving the moment until you experience the wonder of grace.

free samples at the food court

I'M GOING TO CONFESS something to you now.

This . . . is difficult.

It's just that I . . . well . . .

Okay, I'll just say it: I think I may be in love with someone other than my wife.

Who? The person who gives out the free samples in the mall food court.

Let me correct that: *any* person who gives out free samples in the mall food court. Actually, any person who gives out free samples in *any* mall food court.

I haven't gotten to know any of these people, nor have I developed an inappropriate relationship with anyone. I'm not attracted to any of them, but I *am* attracted to the bite-size food they offer me free of charge.

You know what I'm talking about, right? You're walking through the mall. You already ate lunch. But there's a guy standing in front of the Chinese place at the food court. "Would you like a free sample?" he asks. You start to politely decline but then reconsider. "Well, I guess, if it's free."

You find yourself holding a toothpick with a little piece of delicious chicken on it.

I love that chicken and whoever offered it.

You're probably wondering where this is going. I admit, I may be too. But I think it's going to take us someplace. To get there, we need to read 1 Peter 3:15–16.

And if someone asks about your hope as a believer, always be ready to explain it. But do this in a gentle and respectful way. Keep your conscience clear. Then if people speak against you, they will be ashamed when they see what a good life you live because you belong to Christ. (NLT)

I love that. We want people to come to faith in Jesus, because Jesus is the way, the truth, and the life. He is how people live abundant lives now and eternal lives in heaven.

So, how do we help people get there?

The idea in 1 Peter 3:15–16 is that we don't argue people into faith; we *love* people into the faith. Peter gave each of us kind of a sequence to follow: You make Jesus the Lord of your life. You live the way he lived—a life of sacrificial love—even if you must suffer for it.

When you do that, when you show people Jesus like that, they will eventually ask why you live that way and what's different about you. When they do, you—in a gentle, respectful way—share Jesus with them. And, because they've seen your life, the "good life you live because you belong to Christ" (v. 16 NLT)—they will be more open to believing in the Jesus you believe in.

You know what this is kind of like? The free samples at the food court!

Why?

Have you ever had a time when you're walking through the mall and the person from the Chinese food place kind of jumps you: "Hi! Would you like a free sample?"

"Oh! Hello. No. No, thank you. Actually, I already ate lunch. Well, you know, it's free. So, sure, I guess I will take one."

You take the toothpick.

You already ate. You weren't thinking about food. It's a little annoying that this person interrupted you by offering it. But, hey, it's free.

So you eat the little bite and . . . it's good. Really good.

You look at your watch. You do have some time. But you already had lunch.

Well . . . *second lunch!* You buy some chicken.

No one will listen to us if we tell them we're right and that they are wrong and have incomplete lives. *But* if we live good lives, lives of love, it gives them a taste of who God is and of the life he offers us. And, as we humbly hold out Jesus, people will ask. They'll feel like, *I wasn't even thinking about Jesus. Honestly, it's a little annoying to have to, but . . . I don't know, maybe there's something about this.*

You can do that.

With God's help, you can live a good, honorable life of love that shows people Jesus. And if you show people Jesus, you'll get the opportunity to share Jesus.

QUESTION: Consider what the non-Christian people in your life think about you. What is probably the least Christ-like, least attractive thing they notice about you?

CHALLENGE: Whatever that character flaw or sin in your life is, it's time to put it behind you so you can better show people Jesus. So, choose a trusted Christian friend. Get together with them, tell them what you need to change, and ask them for prayer and accountability.

WEEK 7

the practice of
celebrating

[one party at a time]

fight for your right

IN 1986 THE BEASTIE BOYS told everyone to fight for their right to party. Seems a little intense, but I guess they were really into partying.

In Leviticus 23 God told everyone to party or he would kill them. That's very intense, but I guess God is really into partying.

In the Old Testament, God set up a series of annual parties for his people. God's people were to come together to celebrate what he had done *and* what he would do God wanted his people to practice gratitude and live with expectancy.

That's the Old Testament.

In the New Testament, Jesus showed up and fought for his right to party. We repeatedly see Jesus at parties. So much so it led to an accusation the religious leaders made against him: "He's a glutton and a drunkard, and a friend of tax collectors and other sinners!" (Matt. 11:19 NLT).

Jesus also compared God's kingdom to a party and, in a famous trilogy of stories, taught that when someone turns to God a party breaks out in heaven.

Don't miss this: the Bible has a clear and consistent party theology. Could it be we have lost something vital God wants for his people?

It reminds me of what happened a couple years ago after a church service. A guy came up and informed me, "I think somebody should say something to the young man who walked forward wearing a baseball cap. It's really not appropriate to wear that baseball cap in church."

I examined his face to make sure he wasn't joking. He wasn't.

I said, "Oh, you mean the young man who didn't grow up in church but walked forward to give his life to Christ and be baptized? You want me to say something to him about the baseball cap he was wearing?"

He apparently wasn't fluent in sarcasm, because he responded, "Yeah! Somebody should really say something to him."

My adrenaline increased and hit a place where I knew I had to be quiet and walk away. So, I walked away.

I think this upset man represents so many Christians who have lost the celebratory spirit that led God to require partying in the Old Testament and Jesus to repeatedly go to and talk about parties in the New Testament. Party-*less* Christians today may represent the Pharisees in Jesus's day, who'd lost the heart of God and made their faith about keeping rules and traditions. Jesus showed up to destroy what the Pharisees had made of religion. He came and brought partying back.

We need to bring partying back.

Why? Because parties bring joy and we are to practice joy.

> Always be joyful. Never stop praying. Be thankful in all circumstances, for this is God's will for you who belong to Christ Jesus. (1 Thess. 5:16–18 NLT)

God tells us his will for our lives includes *joy*.

Jesus came to bring "great joy" (Luke 2:10) and said he came to fill us with his joy until it overflows (John 15:11).

God's will, the Good News of Jesus, is about joy. Yet this is how someone described to me their understanding of Christianity: "Christianity is the haunting fear that someone somewhere is having a good time." That's the perception a *lot* of people have of Christianity. We've got to put a stop to that.

We need to give people a different view of who Jesus is by giving them a different view of who we are as his followers. Not only because a joyless Christianity misrepresents Jesus and the will of God but also because a joyless

Christianity is unattractive. Jesus didn't draw crowds to himself and impact people one at a time by being joyless. People were drawn to him and will be to us because of *joy*.

Joy is attractive, and parties bring joy.

QUESTION: Why do you think joy is so central to God's will for our lives?

CHALLENGE: Pick three people who know you well. Ask each of them to honestly answer this question: If you had to rate how joyful I seem, on a scale of 1 to 10, what would you say?

What do their answers say to you?

a mattress party

JESUS WAS AT A PARTY.

It didn't feel much like a party.

One of the Pharisees had invited to his home his uptight brood of religious taskmasters, Jesus, and one very out-of-place sick person. The sick guy wouldn't normally have been invited, or even permitted, as the Pharisees thought such people were cursed by God and to be avoided.

So why was he there? It was a trap. The Pharisees knew Jesus was in the habit of healing sick folks. And this "party" was on the Sabbath, so they could use Jesus's "work" of healing on their holy day as an accusation against him.

As expected, Jesus healed the man. This should have been cause for celebrating, and joy should have broken out, but it didn't. The Pharisees smugly felt like they'd caught Jesus.

That's when Jesus picked a fight with them. First, he questioned their thinking that led them to believe sick people shouldn't be healed on the Sabbath. Then he questioned the invite list they used for this party.

> Then Jesus said to his host, "When you give a luncheon or dinner, do not invite your friends, your brothers or sisters, your relatives, or your rich neighbors; if you do, they may invite you back and so you will be repaid. But when you give a banquet, invite the poor, the crippled, the lame, the blind, and you will be blessed. Although they cannot repay you, you will be repaid at the resurrection of the righteous." (Luke 14:12–14)

I don't think Jesus was saying it's wrong to have your friends or family over, but I do believe he was telling the Pharisees that there's no reward in that. What God blesses is inviting people to a party who *need* to be invited to a party.

Did you hear about Mattress Mack? I feel certain that isn't his birth name, but he goes by Mattress Mack. Mack owns huge furniture galleries in Houston. In 2017, when Hurricane Harvey hit the area, there was devastating destruction and flooding. People were desperate, and Mattress Mack opened three of his furniture stores as temporary shelters. In the video footage you can see people—who had lost everything and were quite messy—lying on couches that had $9,000 price tags and sleeping on $6,000 beds.

Mattress Mack didn't just open his stores and wait to see if anyone showed up. He sent out his delivery trucks to areas where he knew there was great need and brought in hurting people who had lost their homes.

Mattress Mack's efforts to help people became national news. A reporter, wanting him to describe what was happening in his furniture galleries, asked, "What's it like?" Mack answered, "Imagine a slumber party on steroids."*

QUESTION: When have you felt desperate and had someone meet a need you had? How did it feel?

CHALLENGE: Who could you work together with (friends from church? your neighbors? your small group?) to throw some kind of party for people who need to be invited to a party? Set up a time to get together and cast a vision for throwing the kind of party described in Luke 14. Pray. Plan it out. Then put on that party!

*Christine Hauser, "'Mattress Mack' Opens Houston Furniture Store as a Shelter," *New York Times*, February 18, 2021, https://www.nytimes.com/2021/02/18/us/mattress-mack-shelter-houston.html.

a mattress party

33

the party planning committee

JESUS WAS WALKING along when he "saw a tax collector by the name of Levi sitting at his tax booth. 'Follow me,' Jesus said to him, and Levi got up, left everything and followed him" (Luke 5:27–28).

Levi, or Matthew as he would more often be called, was a tax collector, which meant he was at the top of everyone's most despised list. Tax collectors were Jews who sided with the occupying and oppressive Roman government. They'd collect taxes from the Jews to give to the Romans. Like mafiosos, tax collectors would also strong-arm the locals into giving them extra money, which they'd put in their own pockets.

Levi was hated, avoided, and declared unclean. The religious leaders wouldn't allow him into the temple. Yet

Jesus came along and invited Levi to be his follower. Levi left everything to follow Jesus.

If you were Levi, what would you do next?

> Then Levi held a great banquet for Jesus at his house, and a large crowd of tax collectors and others were eating with them. (v. 29)

As a follower of Jesus, the most natural thing for Levi was to throw a party. He invited a bunch of his friends who were far from God and he invited Jesus. It was the perfect opportunity for his friends to get a real picture of who Jesus truly was.

The Pharisees were aghast and demanded that Jesus answer their accusing question, "Why do you eat and drink with tax collectors and sinners?" (v. 30).

They didn't understand why Jesus was at a party, especially at a party with *these* people. Jesus answered, "It is not the healthy who need a doctor, but the sick. I have not come to call the righteous, but sinners to repentance" (vv. 31–32).

I love that. It's like, "C'mon. You don't get it? That's why I have come. That's why my followers throw parties, and that's why the invitation list is filled with people who are far from God. What did you expect?"

Throwing a party might be the most natural thing a Christ-follower can do. It might be the most *spiritual* thing a Christ-follower can do.

So, what if *you* threw a party? What kind of party? A party with purpose. A party that will ultimately point people to Jesus.

The idea of it might freak you out a little. I understand. I am not, by nature, a thrower of parties. But good news—it's something that can be *learned*. A missiologist named Hugh Halter, who claims the best way Jesus's followers can help others follow Jesus is by throwing great parties, says, "You have to teach and disciple people in how to throw a good party."*

It's not as difficult as you think. Here are a few ideas:

Greet people at the door.

Show that you are happy to see them.

Smile!

Turn on all your lights—darkness doesn't communicate joy.

Put on some upbeat music—extra points if it's songs your guests already know and probably like.

Offer food—it doesn't have to be fancy, but save the stale half-bag of potato chips for yourself.

Think of something fun you could do together, like play a game, watch a funny video, or perhaps play pin-the-tail-on-your-husband?

*For more on this topic from my friend Hugh, see Hugh Halter, "The Sacrament of Party," Small Groups, accessed May 19, 2021, https://www.smallgroups.com/articles/2017/sacrament-of-party.html.

I bet God is calling you to throw a party, and *I wonder what type of party it is*. Not all parties are the same. I'd encourage you to let your personality and passions guide you. Yours could be hosting a block party cookout for your neighborhood. Playing video games with your friends. Having a surprise appreciation party for the firefighters at your local station. Getting a group together for a *Hot Ones*–style time of eating insanely hot wings and asking each other interview questions. Watching the big finale of your favorite show with a group. Throwing a pool party for everyone on your kid's team. Making a fancy dinner because you're a foodie who loves to cook.

The possibilities are endless, and you can design your party based on the unique way God designed you. The important thing is that your party feature some joy, because joy is part of God's will for your life, and joy points people to Jesus.

QUESTION: What is your favorite party you've ever been to? What made it great?

CHALLENGE: Make a list of party ideas. At this point you're brainstorming—so there are no bad answers. Write down different types of parties you could throw, the people you could invite to each, what could make those parties fun, and so on.

sardines

IN HIS BESTSELLING BOOK *All I Really Need to Know I Learned in Kindergarten*, Robert Fulghum writes about the game hide-and-seek. He bemoans the fact that adults no longer play and that the kids playing outside his window don't knock on his door to invite him. Then he reminisces about playing as a child. He asks,

> Did you ever have a kid in your neighborhood who always hid so good, nobody could find him? We did. After a while we would give up on him and go off, leaving him to rot wherever he was. Sooner or later he would show up, all mad because we didn't keep looking for him. And we would get mad back because he wasn't playing the game that was supposed to be played. There's *hiding* and there's *finding*, we'd say. And he'd say it was hide-and-seek, not hide-and-GIVE-UP.*

*Robert Fulghum, *All I Really Need to Know I Learned in Kindergarten: Uncommon Thoughts on Common Things*, 25th anniversary ed. (New York: Ballantine, 2004), 25.

Fulghum suggests "hide-and-seek-and-yell" might be a better name for the game.

We all know hide-and-seek, but Fulghum goes on to write about a different version of which I was unfamiliar. It's called sardines. One person hides and, after the obligatory count to ten, everyone else goes looking for the one. When they find the hider, they get in and hide with them. "Pretty soon everybody is hiding together, all stacked in a small space like puppies in a pile. And pretty soon somebody giggles and somebody laughs and everybody gets found."†

I've found that's often the way the lost get found in the kingdom of God. I'll ask someone what led them to Jesus, and they'll describe the joy and closeness they discovered in a community of Christians. They realized that these churchgoers weren't what they'd thought. They were not somber rule-keepers. They were people who'd been transformed by the love of God, had become a close-knit spiritual family, and were filled with joy. They enjoyed life and spending time together, and were okay even when times were difficult. This person will pause, remembering what happened, smile, and say, "It was their laughter that drew me in."

I wonder about the party Matthew the tax collector threw.

The Pharisees stood outside, shocked that Jesus was hanging out with Matthew and his sinful friends. How

†Fulghum, *All I Really Need to Know*, 26.

did the Pharisees even become aware that the party was happening? Is it possible they were led to it by the sound of laughter?

I also wonder what happened at the party. These people, all far from God for their own reasons, meeting Jesus for the first time—how shocked were they by him? How attractive was this man, whom they were told represented God, and the way he accepted and embraced them?

The Pharisees asked demanding questions and stormed off at Jesus's audacity in partying with unholy people. But I wonder about how those unholy people walked away from that party. We aren't told, but I bet they were changed. I bet that day some of the lost were found—just like in a successful game of sardines.

QUESTION: Who are some spiritually unengaged people in your oikos? *Oikos* is the Greek word for home or household, but it's sometimes used for people who are close to you, like your family and more intimate friends. What people are pretty close to you but not close to God?

CHALLENGE: Throw an oikos party. An oikos party would be one to which you invite people in your relational network—it might be coworkers, classmates, neighbors, the folks in your fantasy football league, or the parents from your kid's swim lesson group.

Plan out an oikos party that you'll throw in the next month.

egg salad sandwiches and dump's punch

HAVE YOU SEEN THE MOVIE *Because of Winn Dixie?*[*] I don't think it was especially popular, but it was especially beautiful.

The movie is about a young girl named Opal, whose mother walked out when she was three. Now about ten years old, she can no longer remember her mother and is forced to move from town to town because her father's job as a preacher requires it.

Opal is lonely. So is her father, who cries over a picture of his wife every day. Now living in yet another new

[*]*Because of Winn-Dixie*, film, directed by Wayne Wang (Twentieth Century Fox, 2005).

town, Opal meets all kinds of other lonely people: an old blind woman named Gloria who lives by herself in a house deep in the woods, a librarian named Miss Franny who has no family, a bitter man named Mr. Alfred who lives in the mobile home next door, and a misunderstood guitar-playing recluse named Otis.

Opal befriends each of these people, becoming their only friend. She feels empty herself but desperately wants to do something for all her new friends. She says, "I want to help 'em, but I just don't know what to do." Finally, she lands on an idea: she should have a party.

She talks Gloria into helping her, saying, "Miss Franny said the problem with people here is that they forgot how to share their sadness, but what I think is that people forgot how to share their joy. . . . Gloria, we need this party."

She quickly makes a list of all the lonely people she will invite, but Gloria insists that she also include two neighborhood bullies who have made themselves Opal's enemies. Opal agrees.

Everyone is reluctant to come—they're fearful—but eventually they accept the invitation. Soon that old lonely house in the woods is filled with empty people who aren't feeling quite so alone anymore.

The party starts with Gloria, who was probably the most intimidated by the idea of having a party, gathering everyone together to pray. She prays a glorious prayer.

Dear Lord and heavenly Father,

We have egg salad sandwiches, we got Dump's punch, we got pickles, we got doggy pictures, and we have Littmus Lozenges. But, more importantly, dear Lord, we have good friends. Dear Lord, we got good friends to share this warm summer night with us, and for that, we're grateful. Teach us, dear Lord, to love one another. This we ask in your name. Amen.

Soon someone shouts, "Are we havin' a party, or are we havin' a paaaaarrrrrttttttttyy?!"

And Opal says, "My heart doesn't feel so empty anymore. It's full . . . all the way up."

Why? Because of a party. A party that brought lonely people together and filled all of them up

What lonely people has God put around you? It might be a coworker or classmate who is less than popular. Perhaps they often eat alone. Or it could be an elderly person in your neighborhood.

You could also get creative and come up with some lonely people who need some love. Maybe you could go to a nursing home and ask which person never gets visited. Or you could do some research about immigrants who are moving into your community and find ways to connect with them.

God's desire is to "[set] the lonely in families" (Ps. 68:6). He wants to use you to do that. Could you bring some joy to a certain lonely person? Perhaps you could even invite them to a party.

QUESTION: *Xenos* is the Greek word for stranger or foreigner. Who are some xenos God has put in your path or on your heart? They are people you aren't especially close to, perhaps because you just don't know them (yet) or because they're different from you or from a different place than you.

CHALLENGE: Throw a xenos party. God tells us, in Hebrews 13:2: "Do not forget to show hospitality to strangers." "Strangers" comes from that Greek word *xenos*. The original Greek verse actually uses a compound word, *philoxenias*, that has been translated into English as "show hospitality to strangers" but has a more literal translation of "love strangers." We've been commanded to love strangers, and one of the best ways we can do it is by throwing parties and inviting them.

Plan out a xenos party that you will throw in the next two months.

WEEK 8

the practice of
weighing words

[one word at a time]

words create worlds

YOUR WORDS HAVE THE POWER of life and death.

Seem a bit overstated?

I might agree, except it's what God tells us. One word at a time to one person at a time, "The tongue has the power of life and death" (Prov. 18:21).

We speak around sixteen thousand words per day. Granted, some folks skew that number big time. But on average we each speak sixteen thousand words every day. I wonder if the sheer number of words we speak makes it easy to underestimate the significance each word can have. Sixteen thousand words is like writing a sixty-page book every day with the words we speak. And each of those words matters.

So much of loving and impacting people the way Jesus did is about the words we speak. In fact, words create worlds.

God created the world with the power of his words. He literally spoke the world into existence. We're told in Genesis 1 that there was just nothingness until God said, "Let there be light." Boom. Light came. God said it, and it was so. Soon there's a galaxy with an earth filled with water and plants and people. God *spoke* the universe into existence. His words have the power of life.

Then we flip a couple pages in the Bible and see that words also have the power of death. In Genesis 3, sin entered the world. Satan came on the scene in the form of a serpent and got Adam and Eve to rebel against God. How did he do it? He spoke. Satan used words to bring death where there was life and darkness where there was light.

What's interesting is that the serpent's words weren't true, but that didn't keep them from having power. God hardwired the power of words into the universe.

If we turn to the New Testament, we find John introducing Jesus as the Word.

> In the beginning was the Word, and the Word was with God, and the Word was God. He was with God in the beginning. Through him all things were made; without him nothing was made that has been made. In him was life, and that life was the light of all mankind. The light shines in the darkness, and the darkness has not overcome it. (John 1:1–5)

Remember how God spoke light into the darkness of Genesis 1? In John 1 we learn that Jesus *is* the Word God spoke. He is the Word now in human flesh.

Throughout his ministry, we see Jesus using words to bring heaven to earth. He told his disciples he had to go *speak* to people because "that is why I have come" (Mark 1:38).

Jesus began the first recorded teaching we have of his by saying, "The Spirit of the Lord is on me, because he has anointed me to proclaim good news to the poor" (Luke 4:18). Jesus came to *proclaim*, to speak. Of course he did. Because words create worlds.

Jesus constantly used words to speak life and healing and blessing. When he was in a boat and a storm came raging, what did he do? He rebuked the storm. He spoke to it (Mark 4:35–39). He didn't just think the thought, or wrinkle his nose like he was a character in *Bewitched*, or do a "Quit it, now" gesture with his hands. He said, "Peace! Be still!" (v. 39 ESV), and the moment he uttered the words the storm became calm. There was power in his speech.

Jesus arrived at the tomb of his friend Lazarus and raised him from death to life. How? Did he go into the tomb and slap Lazarus on the forehead like some faith healer you might see on TV? Nope. Did he dramatically remove the stone from the tomb like a Las Vegas magician, revealing Lazarus was alive again? Nope. What did

Jesus do? He spoke. He said, "Lazarus, come out!" and Lazarus came out (John 11:43).

If we want to live and love like Jesus, we must understand that words have the power of life and death and start choosing them carefully.

QUESTION: Do you think of your words as being so important? How does it hit you to learn that they are?

CHALLENGE: What if, for five days starting today, you did a "word review" each night? Take a few minutes to prayerfully think through the conversations you had and all the words you spoke. While you do, ask God to help you note any words that might not have been pleasing to him.

dear daughters of God

I UNDERSTAND THE IMPORTANCE of the words I say. I just don't trust myself to say the right ones.

Do you know what I mean? I'm convinced that my words have the power of life and death, which is amazing but also intimidating. Because on my own, I seem to rarely choose the right words.

If you're like me, there's good news. When it comes to choosing the right words, we're not on our own.

Jesus explained that even he got help with his words "These words you hear are not my own; they belong to the Father who sent me" (John 14:24), he said, and he promised help would come for us too. "But the Advocate, the Holy Spirit, whom the Father will send in my name, will teach you all things and will remind you of everything I have said to you" (v. 26). And so we can have confidence because "the Holy Spirit will teach you at that time what you should say" (Luke 12:12).

Have you ever experienced moving out of your comfort zone to love people in Jesus's name and, in a big moment, finding you suddenly had the right words to say?

One time I went to speak at the women's prison in Oldham County, Kentucky. I prayed about what God would want me to say and wrote some notes down on my iPad. But when I pulled into the parking lot, I remembered I wasn't allowed to take any electronics in with me. Uh-oh, my iPad had to stay in the car. Well, like most preachers I have about a half-dozen favorite sermons basically memorized. I figured it was time to pull one of those out of my internal hard drive.

As I was standing in the back of the room during worship, I watched the ladies sing to God. It wasn't difficult to discern that many had lived a very hard life. Several were pregnant. I tried to imagine how lonely it would feel to give birth to a baby and then return to your cell while someone else took care of your newborn. I started praying for them and realized none of my memorized sermons were right for these women. I was minutes away from speaking to them but had no idea what to say.

I was in trouble.

I kept praying and sensed God saying to me, *Kyle, these are my daughters. I love them the way you love your daughters. Make sure they know how I feel about them.* I immediately scrolled through the hard drive in my mind for a talk called "Dear Daughters of God," but I had no such sermon to draw from.

Still in trouble.

When I started walking up to the podium, that's when it happened. The Holy Spirit brought to mind a verse I had memorized eighteen years earlier, Romans 8:16: "The Spirit himself testifies with our spirit that we are God's children." I thought about how the Holy Spirit is constantly reassuring us about our standing with God: through Jesus we are his sons and daughters. I remembered the next verse, Romans 8:17, which speaks of how we have an inheritance that awaits us in heaven—a hope that sustains us through the suffering of this world.

And I had the privilege of telling God's daughters about their Father's love. I could sense the women were attentive, that these were words they needed to hear.

I finished speaking and went back to my seat. The worship leader started leading the response song, and it was "Good Good Father." For the first time I noticed the song sheet that had been handed out at the beginning of the service—this song had been pre-chosen, but I'd had no idea. Do you know the chorus of that song?

"You're a good, good Father. It's who you are. And I'm loved by you. It's who I am."* That was exactly the message I had just shared. It felt . . . prearranged.

I think it was, by our good, good Father.

*Housefires, "Good Good Father," written by Pat Barrett and Anthony Brown, on *Housefires II* (Atlanta: Housefires, 2014), album.

QUESTION: Have you ever avoided a situation or conversation because you were afraid you wouldn't have the right words to say?

CHALLENGE: Your last challenge was to do a daily review of your words each evening. Today's challenge is to start your day—for at least four days starting today—by praying that God will give you the right words to say each time you have a chance to speak into someone's life that day.

what words?

OUR WORDS CREATE WORLDS, so what kind of words should we say?

First, we should speak words of affirmation. Everything we say tears down or builds up, and we need to choose words that build up. God tells us, "Do not let any unwholesome talk come out of your mouths, but only what is helpful for building others up according to their needs, that it may benefit those who listen" (Eph. 4:29).

You speak words of life when you say

to your husband: "I'm so glad I'm married to you. I respect you."

to your wife: "I love you. You are beautiful."

to your kids: "I am so proud of who you are becoming."

to your coworkers: "You are great at what you do."

If you do that, consistently, your words will create worlds. People will start to live up to what you see in them and speak to them.

Second, we should speak words of affection. God does that for us, and we need to do that for each other. God says to us, "I have loved you with an everlasting love" (Jer. 31:3).

There's nothing you could do to make God stop loving you, and he uses words of affection to make sure you know it. We need to let others know we love them with an everlasting love too.

We need to speak words of affection. If that's difficult for you, consider that Jesus taught us, "The mouth speaks what the heart is full of" (Luke 6:45). What comes out of your mouth is a reflection of what's gone into your heart. So, if you struggle to speak loving words of affection, focus on ingesting the loving words of affection God has spoken to you in the Bible.

Third, we should speak words that point people to God. I love how, when people questioned John the Baptist and asked who he was or tried to give him credit, his response was, "I'm not the one. Jesus is the one. I'm here to point people to Jesus" (see John 1:19–34).

As your life looks more like Jesus's, you will receive more compliments. "You're so kind." "I don't know anyone else who listens like you do." "You're always putting other people above yourself." When people ask who you are or try to give you credit, find a humble, not weird, way to point to Jesus. You might say something like, "Wow, thanks. But, honestly, it's not me. It's the impact Jesus has had on my life," or "I appreciate that, but I never used to be that way. It's just, well, I guess spending time with Jesus has kind of rubbed off on me." You might even add, "Did you know Jesus once said, 'Come to me and you will find rest. I'll teach you a new way of doing life'? That's what happened to me."

Fourth, we should speak words to God about people. If we want to have a godly impact on people, we need God's help. We need to pray for and about the people God has put in our lives. "God, help them to see their need for you." "God, what do they need to hear from me? What do I need to say to them?"

And what if you ask the person if you could pray for them or with them? What if you ask a friend or co-worker, "I've started praying for you consistently, and I was wondering, is there anything specific I could be praying for?" What impression might that make?

And what if, instead of arguing with your spouse or your kid, you said, "Let's not fight. Let's pray together and ask God for help"? We're told, in James 4:2, "You quarrel and fight. You do not have because you do not ask God."

I wonder, How many broken relationships would begin healing if we just asked God? How could the future look different from the past if we just asked God? How

what words?

169

many of us would find ourselves using our words to bring life if we just asked God?

We create worlds with our words. Let's create the kind of world God wants and make sure it's one where people know of God and his love.

QUESTION: Ask God, "Who needs to hear from me today?" Who does he put on your heart?

CHALLENGE: Reach out to that person and give some words you believe they need to hear.

i wish you were mine

GOD CHOSE YOU.

Do you know why?

Because he wanted to. God wanted you. He chose to love you. He chose you for relationship with him, to be with him. He chose you to represent and make a difference for him in the world.

I love God's words in Isaiah 43:

> Do not fear, for I have redeemed you;
>> I have summoned you by name; you are mine.
> When you pass through the waters,
>> I will be with you;
> and when you pass through the rivers,
>> they will not sweep over you.
> When you walk through the fire,
>> you will not be burned;

the flames will not set you ablaze. . . .
Since you are precious and honored in my sight,
and because I love you. (vv. 1–2, 4)

God has chosen you! You are his! Is there a better feeling in the world?

On the other hand, is there any pain quite like that of
not being chosen? When you aren't chosen, instead of
feeling like you're seen and belong to someone, you feel
rejected.

Want an incredible one at a time way to change a life?
Let someone know they're chosen. Use your words to do
that.

There's an often-told story told of a girl named Mary
Ann Bird who was born with multiple birth defects,
including a cleft palate. When she started school, her
classmates made fun of her for how she looked. She
said, when schoolmates asked her what happened to her
lip, "I'd tell them I'd fallen and cut it on a piece of glass.
Somehow it seemed more acceptable to have suffered
an accident than to have been born different. I was convinced that no one outside my family could love me."

In second grade, this rejected little girl found herself in
Mrs. Leonard's class. This teacher was short, round, and
happy. The day finally came for the students' annual hearing test.

Mrs. Leonard gave the test to everyone in the class, and finally it was my turn. I knew from past years that as we stood against the door and covered one ear, the teacher sitting at her desk would whisper something, and we would have to repeat it back—things like "The sky is blue" or "Do you have new shoes?" I waited there for those words that God must have put into her mouth, those seven words that changed my life. Mrs. Leonard said, in her whisper, "I wish you were my little girl."*

Wow. With those perfectly chosen words, Mrs. Leonard helped to create a new world for a girl who felt rejected but now had a reason to believe she could be chosen.

That's how God feels about you. He whispers to you, *I wish you were my little one.* If you've given your life to God, if you've allowed him to adopt you, he whispers, *I'm so glad you're my little one.*

That's also how God feels about every person he's put in your life. And God has put those people in your life so you can let them know that they're chosen.

QUESTION: Who do you know who probably needs to hear that God loves them and has chosen them?

*As quoted in "Sermon Illustrations II: Acceptance," Sermon Index, accessed March 14, 2022, https://www.sermonindex.net/modules/articles/index.php?view=article&aid=13959.

i wish you were mine

CHALLENGE: Pray about a way to let someone know they're chosen. It could be very simple. (You don't have to communicate everything a person needs to know at once. People are typically more receptive if it comes little by little.) You might say to (or even text) the person, "Hey. I hope this isn't weird, but I was praying for you and just wanted to make sure you know: God loves you and has chosen you."

a cheap bracelet and some precious words

YOU HAVE NO IDEA how your words can change a life.

Just ask Teddy Stoddard.*

Teddy was a hard boy to like. He slouched in his chair most of the time and spoke only when called upon. He never dressed right. His clothes were always smelly. No one really liked him. Even his fifth-grade teacher, Miss Thompson, got a certain twisted pleasure out of marking his wrong answers. She would put the "F" on top with a flourish. She might have known better, because his history was on record:

*For one telling of this story, see Dahlia Rideout, "Teddy Stoddard, A Touching Story," *More*, accessed February 8, 2022, https://www.more .com/lifestyle/teddy-stoddard-touching-story/.

First grade: "Teddy is a good boy and shows promise but has a poor home situation."

Second grade: "Teddy is quiet and withdrawn. His mother is terminally ill."

Third grade: "Teddy is falling behind. His mother died this year; his father is uninvolved."

Fourth grade: "Teddy is hopelessly backward. His father has moved away; Teddy's living with an aunt. He is deeply troubled."

Then Christmas came, and all the children brought presents for their teacher. Each gift was carefully and festively wrapped, except for Teddy's. His was in a brown paper bag taped sloppily together. He had written on the bag, "For Miss Thompson. From Teddy." When she opened Teddy's present, it was a cheap rhinestone bracelet with most of the stones missing and a bottle of perfume that was mostly empty. The other children started to laugh, but Miss Thompson caught herself. She understood the significance of the moment. Snapping on the bracelet, she said, "Isn't it lovely, class? And doesn't the perfume smell good?"

At the end of class, Teddy approached her shyly. "I'm glad you liked my gifts, Miss Thompson," he whispered. "You smell just like my mom. And her bracelet looked real nice on you too."

After he left, Miss Thompson put her head on her desk and wept. She asked God to forgive her. She prayed that

God would help her to see what he saw when she looked at this motherless boy.

When the children came back to school after the holiday break, Miss Thompson was a changed woman. She spent extra time with the children who needed more help, and Teddy most of all. By the end of the year, he had caught up with most of his classmates and was ahead of some. After that, she didn't hear from him for years.

Then one day she received a note: "Dear Miss Thompson, I wanted you to be the first to know I'm graduating from high school, and I'm second in my class. Love, Teddy Stoddard."

Four years later, another note came: "Dear Miss Thompson, I wanted you to be the first to know I'm graduating first in my class. University has not been easy, but I liked it. Love, Teddy Stoddard."

Four years later, another: "Dear Miss Thompson, I wanted you to be the first to know that as of today I am now Theodore J. Stoddard, MD. How about that? And I've met a girl and I'm getting married. Would you come and sit where my mother would have sat? You're the nearest thing to family that I've ever had. Love, Teddy Stoddard."

And at his wedding she sat where his mother would have sat, wearing that cheap bracelet with many of the stones missing.

I honestly don't know if that's a true story. I hope it is. But either way, the power of the story comes when we apply it to our lives. We all know people who are desperate for love and affirmation. We all have words we can share of love and affirmation. We get to choose if we'll be generous or stingy with those words. The one at a time way of Jesus is to let those words flow.

QUESTION: Can you remember a time when someone said words to you that changed the way you thought of yourself? What happened?

CHALLENGE: Compliment three people today. Ask God to help you see something unique and special about the people he's put in your life, and let at least three of them know what it is.

WEEK 9

the practice of
loving

[one expression at a time]

we love love, but what kind of love?

WE LOVE LOVE. People love the idea of love. You see it everywhere. Half the movies that come out seem to be about people falling in love. People love love movies. Even the Hallmark versions that seem unwatchable to me. But no—if people are falling in love, people love to watch it, no matter how sappy.

You also see it in music. Think of all the songs about love. You've got "All You Need Is Love," "Love Story," "Crazy in Love," "The Power of Love," "When a Man Loves a Woman," "I Just Called to Say I Love You," "Bleeding Love," and "Make You Feel My Love," just to name a few. There's even a "Love Shack." Led Zeppelin would say there's a "Whole Lotta Love."

I suppose that's all good, because love is good, but I wonder. I wonder about how we think of *love* and use the word. For instance, I know a bunch of people who passionately proclaim that they love Diet Coke from McDonald's. Have you met these people? Are you one of these people? They claim there's something different about the Diet Coke at McDonald's and that there are websites that prove it. Talk to them. They'll tell you, "I love Diet Coke from McDonald's!" Other people might say, "I love the pair of boots I just bought," or, "I love my pillow-top mattress," or "I love carne asada."

Again, all good, but it leaves me wondering if we're clear on what it means to love people the way Jesus loved people. I think most of us would say, "I love people." Okay. But is it possible we love only those who are easy to love? Maybe that's who we're talking about when we say we love people?

There are different words in the Bible for love. There's *eros*, which is a love that's based on feeling and is typically used in the context of a romantic or sexual relationship. It's emotional love. I wonder if this is what we mean when we talk about love. It's a feeling we have. It's also a feeling we might not have or could lose. That's why we don't love some people and why we "fall out of love." Because it was just a feeling.

Another word translated "love" in the Bible is *philia*. Philia is a love based on mutual benefits or commonality and is often used in the context of friends or family members. It's good—like "brotherly love"—but can be conditional. It can be a "We love each other because of what we do for each other" kind of love.

The word *agape* is also translated "love" in the Bible. Agape is love that is selfless, sacrificial, and unconditional. It's a love that loves even when nothing is offered in return.

When we read about God's love for us in the Bible, it's agape love. It's agape love that leads God to send Jesus to the world to save us. When did Jesus die for us? We read in Romans 5 that it was "when we were still powerless," and when we were "ungodly" and "God's enemies" (vv. 6, 10). And verse 8 explains, "But God demonstrates his own love for us in this: While we were still sinners, Christ died for us."

That's the kind of love God loves us with, and it's the kind of love he calls us to love others with.

We love the idea of loving people. It sounds great. The issue is that some of the people we need to love are incredibly difficult to love. We wonder if maybe loving people has its limits. No. It doesn't for God. He loves us at our worst. He doesn't wait for us to apologize or change our ways. He does everything for us—he gives us his Son—when we are his enemies.

That's the kind of love we're to give to others.

It's the kind of love people notice. And the kind of love that changes a person's life.

QUESTION: When you think about God loving you and Jesus dying for you, do you typically think about yourself at your very worst and as an enemy of God? How might realizing that help you to feel more loved by him, in a life-changing way?

CHALLENGE: Make a "hard for me to love" list. The idea of this list isn't to re-feel your negative feelings but to ask God to help you search your heart so you can see where you're off course. As you put down each person or group of people, ask God to help you identify the true reasons you struggle to love them and to help you repent so you start loving them the way he loves you.

what is it like to love you?

JESUS SAID TO LOVE YOUR ENEMY, to love those who are hard to love. So, who do you need to love?

For you it might be . . .

The parent who abused you.

The boss who comes at you with never-ending negativity, nagging, and nitpicking.

The schoolyard bully who called you names that you're tempted to continue to let define you to this day.

The martyr who is forever the victim, always making sure you know how unfairly life has treated them.

The "friend" who always has to be in the spotlight, always exaggerates, and has created a photoshopped life on social media.

The ex who broke your heart.

Who is hard for you to love?

I think of the guy who came over to talk to me one Thursday when I was sitting in a local café. I'd been working on my computer, writing my sermon for that weekend. He casually put his wow-that's-really-a-grande ridiculously large coffee next to my computer and then accidently knocked it over right onto it.* My computer just blinked out.†

He went to grab some napkins as I had an out-of-body moment. I thought, *Wait, is this real? Is this happening?* then grabbed my computer and started to run. The coffee was pouring out of my computer and down my arms. I had third-degree burns but I didn't care; I was running. I didn't know where I was running to, but I knew I had to try to save my computer *and* that this was definitely a man I would *never* love.

Who have you decided you will never love?

Will you choose, in Jesus's name, to love that person? Loving someone who doesn't deserve love from you may be the most powerfully impactful thing you can do.

Perhaps a better question than if you *will* love that person is, *How* will you be able to love that person? Think of the leper who asked Jesus to heal him and said, "Lord, if you are willing" (Matt. 8:2). He knew Jesus was able; he just wasn't sure Jesus was *willing*. You may be willing to

*I'm giving him the benefit of the doubt and assuming it was an accident.
†"Blinked out" may not be the technical name for what happened.

love someone difficult but not sure if you're able. It's not easy, so what will enable you to do this?

I have two questions I've learned to ask myself that help me.

Let's begin with this one: *What is it like for God to love me?* We're told in 1 John 4:19, "We love because he first loved us."

That's so important. It means we don't manufacture love. The way to grow in love isn't to summon up loving feelings. The way to grow in love is to be loved. We receive God's love, we're filled with it, and it starts to ooze out of us. We don't conjure up love; we're conduits of it. We get better at loving by better understanding and experiencing God's love.

So, what is it like for God to love me?

I've found that I'm really good at *not* feeling really sinful. I have a way of excusing my sin, of using the circumstances of my life to rationalize who I am and what I've done. But the truth is that I'm a sinner who has lived my life in rebellion against God. The apostle Paul described himself as "the worst of sinners" (1 Tim. 1:16), and on my more honest days, I get that. I feel like I could compete for that top spot.

You are a sinner too. In fact, you might be surprised to discover that you're in the running for "worst." You've lived your life in a daily uprising against God's leadership so you could take over, be your own god, and do whatever you want to do.

And yet God loves you. He loves you despite you. He loves you more than you'd dare to imagine.

When you realize how hard you are to love, but that even still God loves you, it makes more sense for you to love someone who is hard to love.

QUESTION: What do you think it's like for God to love you?

CHALLENGE: Memorize a Bible verse about God's love for you. Perhaps Romans 5:8 or 1 John 3:1, "See what great love the Father has lavished on us, that we should be called children of God!" Or 1 John 4:16, "And so we know and rely on the love God has for us. God is love."

what is it like to be them?

HOW WILL YOU BE ABLE to love someone who is hard to love?

As I mentioned yesterday, I've found two helpful questions to ask myself. Yesterday I shared the first: *What is it like for God to love me?* Here's the second: *What is it like to be them?*

In the first church I ever preached at, there was a seven year old boy who came by himself every Sunday. His name was Randy. He didn't live too far away, and his parents would send him on his own. Randy was out of control. He would run around yelling and punching. There were only about fifty people in the entire church, so Randy was pretty noticeable. I tried to be patient with him, but eventually I was done. Randy was at the top of my hard to love list.

Then came the fateful Sunday when I was preaching and saw Randy running around in the foyer. There were glass doors between the sanctuary and the lobby. Randy stopped running, took a Matchbox toy car, and chucked it at the door. The glass shattered. Everyone was startled, and I was furious. After the service, I marched Randy back to his home, because I was going to tell his mom and dad that he could no longer come without supervision.

We arrived at his house, which was an old, rundown, maybe five-hundred-square-foot singlewide trailer. His mom stepped out, saw me with her son, and yelled, "What did that blankety-blank do now?" She grabbed him by the arm and yanked him inside, cussing the whole time and telling me how hard her life was because of this blankety-blank kid. I walked through the door and saw a couch with a stained pillow and blanket on it. I realized, *This is where Randy sleeps. This is his room.* His mom was still cursing, and it quickly became obvious Randy had no dad in his life.

I was abruptly overwhelmed with the question, *What is it like to be Randy?* I couldn't even imagine, and I felt a flood of compassion. In that moment, I had nothing but love for this boy who had always been so hard to love.

I said to his mom, "I just wanted to tell you that you've got a special one here. You're always welcome to come to church with him, but we're sure glad he comes every week."

What if, with that person who is so hard to love, you ask yourself, *What is it like to be them?* Take your eyes off yourself for a second and prayerfully wonder, *What is it like to grow up with an abusive parent like they did? What is it like to have to deal with that disability? What is it like to have your spouse cheat on you and leave? What is it like to be a single parent with those pressures?*

What is it like? Ask the question, and compassion will start to grow.

QUESTION: You've made a list of people whom you find difficult to love. Look at those names and prayerfully ask, "What's it like to be them?"

CHALLENGE: You've memorized a verse about God's love for you. Now memorize a verse about God's call for you to love others. How about, "Dear friends, let us love one another, for love comes from God. Everyone who loves has been born of God and knows God. Whoever does not love does not know God, because God is love. . . . Dear friends, since God so loved us, we also ought to love one another" (1 John 4:7–8, 11) Or maybe John 13:34–35: "A new command I give you: Love one another. As I have loved you, so you must love one another. By this everyone will know that you are my disciples, if you love one another."

44

touch

THERE'S A SONG BY MUDHONEY, a little-known '90s Seattle grunge band, called "Touch Me, I'm Sick."

I don't know anything about the band, but I think their song title expresses the silent cry of nearly every person. We may not admit them, but we know our ugly thoughts and desires. We know how even the good things we do are often corrupted by selfish motives. Deep down, we know we're sick.

And we long for someone to understand and still love us. We crave compassion. We're desperate for healing. We echo those words. *Touch me. I'm sick.*

Jesus changed lives, one at a time, by touching the sick.

Jesus calls us to change lives, one at a time, by touching the sick.

When I think of someone touching the sick, my mind goes to Mother Teresa. She spent her life ministering to the least of the least in the gutters of Calcutta, India. It changed the lives of those she touched but also of those who looked on at her love. Once I heard a story about a Muslim cleric who came and watched for the longest time as she washed a leper. He said afterward, "All these years, I have believed that Jesus was a prophet. But today I believe Jesus Christ is God, if he is able to give such joy to this sister, enabling her to do her work with so much love."

Over the years, many people came to speak with her, to attempt to figure out what motivated her and discover what special abilities she had that enabled her to achieve such an impact and to persevere in such difficult, seemingly thankless, and endless work.

Her answer? She had no special gift. It wasn't her work at all. In an interview with Edward Desmond, a reporter from *Time* magazine, she said, "I don't claim anything of the work. It is [God's] work. I am like a little pencil in his hand. That is all. He does the thinking. He does the writing. The pencil has nothing to do with it. The pencil has only to be allowed to be used."

Mother Teresa devoted her life to touching the sick not because she was talented but because she wanted to be with her Jesus. She told the reporter that she began each day with prayer, rising at 4:30 a.m. From there, she continued to pray throughout her day, saying she would "try to pray through [my] work by doing it with Jesus, for Jesus, to Jesus."

Doing so, she said, helped her put her whole heart and soul into her work, and helped her see that each person she touched was "Jesus in disguise." Each unwanted, unloved, and unwashed person was a gift. An opportunity to be "24 hours a day with Jesus."*

Mother Teresa knew that when she loved others in Jesus's name, he was right there with her. She also knew that Jesus said, "Truly I tell you, whatever you did for one of the least of these brothers and sisters of mine, you did for me" (Matt. 25:40). So, when she was loving someone in Jesus's name, she was loving Jesus.

QUESTION: When we talk about "touching" someone, we obviously don't just mean physical touch. What are some different ways you could touch someone who might be hurting, lonely, or in need?

CHALLENGE: There are probably several people whom you could touch in a meaningful way. Ask God who most needs your touch right now and what the most powerful way to touch them would be. Whatever God tells you, do it.

*Edward W. Desmond, "Interview with MOTHER Teresa: A Pencil in the Hand of God," *Time*, December 4, 1989, http://content.time.com /time/subscriber/article/0,33009,959149-1,00.html.

DAY 45

three miles per hour

ONE REASON WE FIND IT HARD to love is because so often we are in a hurry. It's hard to love in a hurry.

I speak from experience, because I'm always in a hurry. When they were young, if you'd asked my kids what a yellow light meant, they would not have said, "Slow down and be careful." They would've said, "Hurry up! Get through it!" because that's how I approach yellow lights.

If you asked them how many times you need to push the elevator button, they would not have said, "Once," though it's obviously the correct answer. They would've said, "Over and over. At least three or four times," because if the elevator door doesn't open instantly, I just keep hitting that button.

I seem to always be in a hurry. But I've noticed Jesus was *never* in a hurry. I've read the Gospels countless times and not yet found the place where Jesus says, "Guys! We've gotta hustle! Let's move!" Jesus never rushed. I drive as fast as I can in my car. Jesus walked slowly. And I think it was because of what was most important to him.

When someone asked Jesus to pinpoint the most important commandment, Jesus answered, "Okay, here it is: love God," and then he added, "Actually, I'll give you two commandments. The first priority is to love God; the second is to love people." Then he said, "Do this and you will live" (see Luke 10:27–28).

I love that. "Do this and you will live." I'm quite sure the people listening to Jesus were alive when he spoke those words. He wasn't addressing dead people. He looked out at a bunch of living people and let them know, "If you want to really live, you have to really love God and love people."

At its core, the Jesus life is about loving God and loving people. And it's impossible to love God or people in a hurry. Some of us are living too fast to really live. That's why Jesus walked slowly. So he could love.

Theologian Kosuke Koyama wrote,

> God walks "slowly" because he is love. If he is not love he would have gone much faster. Love has its speed. It is an inner speed. It is a spiritual speed. It is a different kind of speed from the technological speed to which we are accustomed. . . . It goes on in the depth of our life, whether we notice or not, whether we are currently hit by storm

or not, at three miles an hour. It is the speed we walk, and therefore it is the speed the love of God walks.*

QUESTION: When have you missed out on an opportunity to love someone because you were in too much of a hurry to live out your own agenda?

CHALLENGE: One of the reasons we're always in such a hurry is because we have so much to do. You probably have a long to-do list. Today, create a "to-don't" list. What are a couple things you could stop doing or reduce the amount of time you spend doing? How could you set yourself up to be able to move slower?

*Kosuke Koyama, *Three Mile an Hour God* (repr. London: SCM Press, 2015).

WEEK 10

the practice of
connecting

[one conversation at a time]

privacy, privacy, privacy

WE HAVE A MISSION. We need to connect with people and help them get connected with God. Every person you see is a child of God. They're all either found or lost sons and daughters of God. If they're lost, they desperately need their heavenly Father, and their heavenly Father desperately wants them.

We connect with people. They get connected to God.

For that to happen, conversations need to happen. And at some point, we need to have a spiritual conversation with the person.

The idea of that can feel intimidating. In fact, a lot of Christians will do almost anything to get out of having a conversation about Jesus with a nonbeliever.

Years ago, my wife agreed to watch someone's dog while they were away. I was not consulted. I came home and discovered a strange dog in our house. I walked in. I saw the dog. The dog saw me. The dog peed. The dog ran away. It is . . . unusual to walk into your house and be greeted by an unexpected urinating dog. My wife explained that we were dog-sitting *and* that the dog was scared of men. Which meant—yes, you probably guessed it—*every* time the dog saw me it would pee and run.

I think that's how a lot of us can be about having "Jesus conversations" with people. Well, minus the pee. Too often, we run from them.

Let's stop running. Because influence comes through conversations. Jesus knew this. In the Bible, we see Jesus speaking to crowds only fifteen times but having *forty* one-on-one conversations.

If we let fear stop us, we'll miss out on the impact God intends for us to have.

I'm convinced that God has *you* in the home you're in so you can bring Jesus to your neighborhood. He has you in your job so you can be a missionary to that workplace. The person checking you out at the grocery store, or sitting next to you on the airplane, or waiting on you at the restaurant, is not random but a divine appointment God has provided you. We don't want to get to the end of our lives and realize we missed out on the influence God intended for us because we ran from conversations he wanted us to have.

Will it always go great? Probably not always.

Some years ago, my family moved into a new neighborhood. We'd only been there a few days when I saw my neighbor across the street mowing his yard. I thought, *This is a good opportunity for me to go over and introduce myself and meet my neighbor.* I walked over to him, and he turned his mower off. I said hi and introduced myself. I told him, "This looks like a great neighborhood. We're excited to live here!"

He said— and you're not going to believe me, but I promise this is a direct quote—"Oh, I love this neighborhood. My three favorite things about this neighborhood are privacy . . . privacy . . . privacy." He then turned his mower back on, and I walked back across the street. *That went well.*

That neighbor wasn't open to *any* conversation. And we fear our friends won't be open to a spiritual conversation and will reject us. But the truth is, most people *are* open. Way more open than we assume. That's especially true if you've been living out these one at a time practices. Praying for that person, showing them love and compassion, inviting them over for a meal or a party—all of it opens them to connecting with you and ultimately with God.

QUESTION: When was the last spiritual conversation you had with someone who was far from God? How did it go?

CHALLENGE: We often let our fear speak to us, but we don't speak to our fear. Take a few minutes to prayerfully think about any fear that might lead you to avoid spiritual conversations. Ask yourself, *What is my fear telling me? What's really at the root of it? Why am I really afraid?* Then ask, *What's the worst that can happen?* Don't let your fear carry you away with imaginary nightmare scenarios. Ask God to help you come up with the true answer. Then courageously speak back to your fear with that truth.

excuses

JESUS'S CONVERSATION with the Samaritan woman in John 4 never should've happened.

Why?

For one, Jesus spoke with a woman. At that time, men and women rarely conversed. Husbands didn't even talk to their wives in public.

Not only was she a woman but one most everyone would overlook. Actually, she was a woman many would intentionally avoid. She had a sordid past, and being seen with her could damage a person's reputation.

Also, she was a *Samaritan* woman. Jesus was Jewish, taught his entire life that good Jews didn't interact with people of the despised Samaritan race.

This conversation also could've been missed because Jesus was tired and hungry. His disciples went off in search of food while he sat down by a well to rest. I don't know about you, but when I'm hangry, the *last* thing I want is to have a deep, important conversation with a stranger.

There were all kinds of reasons this conversation shouldn't have happened, and all kinds of ways Jesus could've justified not having it.

We tend to find all kinds of reasons why we can't have spiritual conversations. Maybe you've thought, *I can't do that because my life isn't a good enough example.* Or, *I can't share Jesus because I'm not very good at it.* Or, *I can't talk about my faith because I wouldn't know what to say.* Or, *I can't tell people about Jesus because I wouldn't know the answers to their questions.*

Do you notice the common theme in all those reasons? "I."

All those excuses are about *you.* And they're all illegitimate, because it's not about you. You don't lead people to Jesus. God does. You *do* have a part to play. You get to have conversations about Jesus. But you can't lead a person to Jesus. God does that. So, don't worry that you can't do it right or don't have the right words. You do your best at your part, and God will do his part of leading the person to Jesus.

The other objection we have to spiritual conversations is fear of how people will react. But if we do this the way Jesus did, we'll discover that almost everyone is more open than we might imagine.

And we can overcome the fear. Did you know there are countries around the world today where people get killed for talking about Jesus but don't let that stop them? In one Muslim nation, for example, when a certain missionary leads people to faith, he has them make a list of everyone they know who isn't a Christian. (This list typically includes everyone they know.) The missionary then has the new Christian circle the names of the ten people who would be least likely to kill them for talking about Jesus. The new Christian is then encouraged to share Jesus with those ten people as soon as possible. *And they do it.* They must be afraid, but they overcome the fear.

We need to let our love for God and our concern for people overcome our excuses. I know a pastor who asks people, "If I paid you $10,000 for every time you told someone about your faith in Jesus, would you do it? Would you start looking for every possible opportunity to have spiritual conversations? Probably so. Why? Because we care enough about money to overcome our fear and our excuses. We need to care more about God and people than we do about money."

With God's help, we can overcome our excuses and our fear.

QUESTION: If someone asked you why you haven't recently had a bunch of conversations about Jesus with people who don't believe in Jesus, what would you answer?

CHALLENGE: Jesus gave us the mission of sharing the Good News. We need to obey him and live out our purpose. Understanding that you don't do this alone but in partnership with God, start making this something you pray about every day. Pray that God will help you overcome your fear, give you opportunities, and empower you to have amazing spiritual conversations.

48

Godportunities

HERE'S A LITTLE A + B = C. Ready?

(A) God wants his lost children to come home. He wants to use you to let them know God loves them and is inviting them.

(B) God is sovereign. He knows all and can control circumstances. And so . . .

(C) God will set up divine appointments where you have what may feel like "chance encounters" with people through which you can graciously point them to Jesus.

We need to look for these Godportunities (yes, I made that word up just now) and be ready when they happen.

I am *not* suggesting that you manufacture awkward conversations. I don't think it's especially effective to approach a stranger with, "Hi, nice to meet you. Do you know Jesus as your Lord and Savior?" or, "Excuse me, sir, can I share the gospel with you? Sir? Wait! Sir!" If we're bold in a way that feels obnoxious, it can do more damage than good.

I *am* suggesting we look for opportunities God gives us to share Jesus. Typically, these will involve people with whom you already have a relationship. When you have established your character, it builds trust and earns you the right to be heard. But God may sometimes set up a divine appointment for you with a stranger. Either way, we need to be on the lookout for these Godportunities.

Think about Jesus and the Samaritan woman. Was it just a coincidence that she walked up to the well where Jesus was sitting?

Or in Acts 16, we see Paul felt led to Philippi. We don't know what he was expecting, but he was arrested and thrown in jail. I bet that's *not* what he expected. Perhaps he felt let down because he wasn't free to preach the gospel to all the people in Philippi. But Jesus's way is one at a time, and in prison Paul was able to have a spiritual conversation with the jailer. The jailer came to faith, and then his whole family joined him in believing in Jesus and getting baptized.

Earlier in this book, we read about Philip meeting an Ethiopian eunuch on a lonely road. The Ethiopian was reading the Old Testament, trying to understand God and his offer of salvation, when Philip approached him and struck up a conversation. Then, Acts 8 says,

Philip began with that very passage of Scripture and told him the good news about Jesus. As they traveled along the road, they came to some water and the eunuch said, "Look, here is water. What can stand in the way of my being baptized?" (vv. 35–36)

Wow, what a crazy story!

And God wants to give you some crazy stories too. How can you increase your chances of being involved in some?

1. Pray for divine appointments. Ask God to give them to you.
2. Prepare for divine appointments. Ready yourself and be on the lookout for them.
3. Pounce on divine appointments. When a Godportunity presents itself, act on it. It may become one of the most exciting and fulfilling experiences you've ever had.

QUESTION: Have you ever had a coincidence that was so special it seemed as if God had to be involved in it? God is sovereign, all-knowing, and all-powerful. He wants to bless both us and other people. If we're willing to let the Holy Spirit lead us, great things are possible.

CHALLENGE: For a week (but this may be something you want to keep doing), during each interaction with someone (including servers, cashiers, etc.), say, "I hope this isn't weird, but I like to pray for people, and I was wondering if there's anything I could be praying for you?" Take note of the person's prayer request but also be ready for your question to initiate a spiritual conversation.

the nudge

JESUS WAS TRAVELING from city to city and we're told, "He had to go through Samaria" (John 4:4).

As we talked about earlier, "had to go" makes it sound like a geographical necessity, but it wasn't. In fact, "through Samaria" was the one way Jewish people would *not* go. Instead, they would go through Perea by crossing over the Jordan. It was longer but avoided the spiritual defilement of entering Samaria.

Jesus *had to* go through Samaria not because of geography but because of a woman who lived there. I wonder if maybe Jesus's original plan was to take the well-traveled route through Perea but, as he prayed that morning, he felt a nudge from God. *Go through Samaria.*

Have you ever felt that nudge? Maybe God impressed on you that there was an old friend you needed to check in with, a coworker you should talk to, or a family member you had to call.

Better question: Do you pray for that nudge? I have a pastor friend who encourages his church to pray each morning, "God, how do you want to love me today, and who do you want to love through me today?"

Do you ask God for divine appointments?

Jesus seeks out this woman who is far from God because he wants everyone to be close to God. We need to do the same.

It may be a challenge, because the longer you're a Christian, the less likely you are to spend time with non-Christians. Joe Aldridge has done extensive research on this, and he tells us that after being a Christian for two years the average follower of Jesus no longer has a single significant relationship with a nonbeliever.* This happens because Christians spend so much of their time with their Christian friends and at church events. I've heard this called "Rabbit Hole Christianity," because the only time Christians are around non-Christians is when they pop out of their Christian hole and make a mad dash to some other Christian event.

We need to get close to people who are far from God. Why? Because we love God. Because he loves us. And because

> Christ's love compels us, because we are convinced that
> one died for all, and therefore all died. And he died for all,

*Joe Aldridge, *Lifestyle Evangelism: Learning to Open Your Life to Those around You* (Colorado Springs: Multnomah Books, 1981).

that those who live should no longer live for themselves
but for him who died for them and was raised again.
(2 Cor. 5:14–15)

Because God wants us to connect with people who are far from him, and because Christ's love compels us, God will nudge us to reach out to a specific person for a spiritual conversation.

When that nudge happens, I encourage you to do what God is calling you to do *immediately*. The moment you know what God wants you to do is the moment to do it. If he nudges you to call someone or help someone or share your faith with someone, that's not something for you to consider. It's something to do . . . now. But too often, instead of obeying instantly, we pause. We wonder if it's really God. We question whether it's the best thing to do. We come up with some other options.

No. We can't pause. Pausing eliminates confidence.

Studies of the thinking process of firefighters have raised interesting conclusions. Researchers try to determine how firefighters are able to make such critical decisions in the heat of crisis at blinding speed. A bad decision would cost them or others their lives. Yet time and time again the best firefighters just seem to know what to do. What's been discovered is that these firefighters aren't weighing multiple options at one time. They're not evaluating various scenarios and then choosing the best one. They are acting on their first thoughts. They have absolute confidence in their instincts. They don't wait long enough for a second option to emerge. They've developed an intuition that allows them to move without hesitation and with the greatest effectiveness.

The first time they are in a fire, they don't have the fully honed instincts to immediately make the right choice, but each fire they experience further develops their ability to do the right thing immediately.

The path to courage is to do the right thing immediately. When you feel the nudge, do it. Each time you pause, you're training yourself to hesitate, to consider your options, to weigh the cost, to fear the consequences, to say no to God.

So, don't pause. When you feel the nudge from God, do it. Immediately.

QUESTION: When have you felt a nudge from God but ignored it? What regrets do you have about maybe missing out on being part of an amazing story?

Have you had a time when you felt the nudge and followed it? If so, what happened?

CHALLENGE: Be sensitive to receiving a nudge from God. When he gives you one, don't question it—do whatever you feel God is nudging you to do *immediately*.

what do i say?

WE NEED TO CONNECT with people so they might connect with God. That happens through conversations.

Okay. Sounds good. But what do you say in one of these conversations?

That's a great question.

Here's some good news: there is no one right way to tell people about Jesus. Whew! That means you don't have to be afraid of getting it wrong.

If you read through the book of Acts, you'll see several people share their faith and discover there isn't a standard way to present Jesus. Different people did it in different ways. In fact, the same person would do it in different ways when speaking to different audiences.

So, if you think you don't know the "right way" to do it, well, no problem. There is no right way to do it. The early Christians we read about in Acts, instead of having some manufactured, memorized speech to give everyone, tried to meet people where they were and then walk them toward God and faith in Jesus.

We do the same. We meet people where they are and make sure what we say makes sense. We don't use religious language like, "That's when I was washed in the blood of the Lamb." And we don't show off the Bible words we know: "And you, too, can experience justification."

No, we just talk in everyday language and try to make it as simple as we can.

You might say, "There's a God who loves you. And you may have walked away from him, but he's never stopped loving you. And he sent Jesus for you. He's inviting you to come back to him. To have a relationship with him that will give you a better life now and life with him forever in heaven." You could say that!

Or you could tell the story of the prodigal son: "A loving father had two sons. One of them basically tells his dad that he wishes him dead, but since his dad wasn't, he at least wanted his share of the inheritance so he could leave home and never come back. The father is so gracious he agrees and gives his son half his money. The son goes off and lives a wild life, rebelling against everything his father stood for and taught him. Eventually he bottoms out. He realizes he had it so much better at home. He decides to return but assumes his father would never accept him as a son. He plans on begging his dad to hire him to work in his fields. But it turns out that, ever since the son left, the father has been sitting on the front porch waiting for his son to come home. When the father sees him in the distance, he runs to him, hugs him, forgives him, and welcomes him back into the family. Jesus told that story and said the father represents God. God loves you even if you've rejected him, and he wants you to come home to a relationship with him."

You could say that! Or you could use a Bible and simplify your explanation to one verse. Romans 6:23 is a great option: "For the wages of sin is death, but the gift of God is eternal life in Christ Jesus our Lord."

You walk through that verse with your friend, perhaps saying something like, "It says 'the wages.' What's a wage? It's something you earn. The wages 'of sin.' What's sin? It's when we do wrong . . . live in a way that's not loving . . . dishonor God. It says the wages of sin 'is death.' What's death? It's an ending . . . an unwanted separation . . . the end of relationship. So, what we've earned through our sin is death.

"Then it says, 'But the gift of God.' What's a gift? It's something we're given that we haven't earned. Something that someone who loves us gives us, just because they love us. And it says God is offering each of us a gift.

"What is it? 'Eternal life.' What's that? It's life without end . . . without separation. It's life where relationship, specifically with God, doesn't end. How is this possible?

That's the next phrase, 'in Christ Jesus our Lord.' The idea is that this is only possible because of Jesus. Because when Jesus died, he took what we deserved by taking away our sin. And he made it possible for God to offer us the gift of eternal life. And that gift is available to you if you just say yes."

You could say that!

There are different ways you can explain it. The key is to keep it simple and present it graciously.

QUESTION: How will you explain the gospel when given the opportunity?

CHALLENGE: Present the gospel to someone this week. Think of all the people God has put in your life. Who do you assume is most ready to hear it? Ask that person to get together (coffee? lunch?), and while you're together ask for permission to share. It might be something like, "I know you know I'm a Christian, but I've never shared what I believe. Would it be okay with you if I did?" If your friend says yes, go for it! Be gracious, keep it pretty short, and make it personal (add a personal element, like why you believe or how Jesus has changed your life).

WEEK 11

the practice of
listening

[one meal at a time]

meals heal

MEALS HEAL.

Yes, that rhymes, and I get a bonus from the publisher for each rhyme I put in the book.* But it more than rhymes; it's a powerful truth we have at our disposal as followers of Jesus trying to live out his one at a time lifestyle.

Eating with another person creates a connection.

(I would say, "Eating another person creates a controversy," but I don't get a bonus from the publisher for each reference to cannibalism I put in the book.)

We see in the Gospels that sharing meals creates opportunities for fostering unity and connecting with people who are different. Something happens when we share a meal. Many of Jesus's amazing one at a time stories involve him eating with others. And one of the most common accusations the religious leaders made against Jesus was that he ate with people who were unclean

*That may not be true.

sinners, outcasts, and outsiders. If you don't look for it you might not notice it, but when Jesus was connecting with people, it was often over a meal.

In Scripture, God is most consistently described as *Father*. He is a perfect heavenly Father. He looks at a world filled with his kids he loves, whom he deeply desires would love each other. As a father, it grieves him to see his kids turn on each other and be divided over so many things. Politics. Race. Social status. Religion. Creamy or crunchy peanut butter.

How does it feel to be the father of seven billion kids who can't get along? To make it worse, sometimes the separation between people can keep people separated from God.

So, what's the solution for the walls that have been built up and the barriers that separate us?

Food.

I'm aware of "foodies" who have refined taste and enjoy trying new gourmet restaurants and dishes. Me? I like hot dogs. Pigs in a blanket especially. It's a little more high-class if you wrap a biscuit around the hot dog.

Yeah, I'm not a food connoisseur or authority, but I do know this: meals heal. There's something that happens around a table. Eating together brings people together. A shared meal has a way of leading to shared life. One of the most effective ways to influence someone is over one meal at a time.

With a meal, there may be awkwardness over the appetizers, but by the main course we're having meaningful conversation. We move from talking about what's going on with the weather to what's going on in our lives. We're not just sharing food; we're sharing needs and dreams and concerns. Eventually, a meal will provide an opportunity to connect with someone and share what Jesus has done in our lives in an unforced way. Meals offer a uniquely relaxed setting in which to ask questions and to listen.

Breaking bread breaks barriers.

Meals heal.

QUESTION: When have you gotten to know someone or had barriers broken over a meal?

CHALLENGE: Invite someone at your work or school to eat lunch with you. Over lunch, ask a bunch of questions. None have to be faith-related. Just have fun getting to know the person.

DAY 52

please, God, let me listen

I THINK MEALS are powerful in large part because they provide an opportunity to listen. You're sitting there together for thirty, sixty, ninety minutes. You talk. The other person talks, and you listen. You ask some questions. They ask some questions. You both talk some more.

If not, you'll just be hearing each other chew. Gross. Listening is huge.

In Dietrich Bonhoeffer's classic book *Life Together*, he has a section on the "ministry of listening." According to Bonhoeffer, there are many times when "listening can be a greater service than speaking." He wrote, "We should listen with the ears of God that we may speak the Word of God."*

*Dietrich Bonhoeffer, *Life Together* (New York: Harper & Row, 1954), 98.

Unfortunately, we don't always have God's heart, and so we don't listen with his ears. We find it hard to listen because listening is caring for the other person, and it's so easy to care mostly about ourselves.

Bonhoeffer also wrote about what he calls "a kind of listening with half an ear."† You know what he means. So do I. It's when I'm sitting on the couch watching football and my wife comes in, talks to me, and then says, "Did you hear what I said?" And I say, "Yes, of course" very indignantly.

But then she asks, "Okay, what did I say?"

"Something . . . about . . . the sink? Or a drink?"

Half-ear listening is not really listening. Bonhoeffer described it as "impatient, inattentive listening" that "despises the brother and is only waiting for a chance to speak and thus get rid of the other person."

Having God's heart allows us to really listen and, as Bonhoeffer said, "Often a person can be helped merely by having someone who will listen to him seriously."‡

Erma Bombeck wrote about a time she got dropped off at the airport and got to her gate a half hour early:

> [At last] there were thirty whole beautiful minutes before my plane took off—time for me to be alone with my own thoughts, to open a book and let my mind wander. A

† Bonhoeffer, *Life Together*, 98.
‡ Bonhoeffer, *Life Together*, 99.

voice next to me belonging to an elderly woman said, "I'll bet it's cold in Chicago."

Stone-faced, I answered, "It's likely."

"I haven't been to Chicago in nearly three years," she persisted. "My son lives there."

"That's nice," I said, my eyes intent on the printed page of the book.

"My husband's body is on this plane. We've been married for fifty-three years. I don't drive, you know, and when he died a nun drove me from the hospital. We aren't even Catholic. The funeral director let me come to the airport with him." . . .

I don't think I have ever detested myself more than I did at that moment. Another human being was screaming to be heard and in desperation, had turned to a cold stranger who was more interested in a novel than in the real-life drama at her elbow. All she needed was a listener—no advice, wisdom, experience, money, assistance, expertise or even compassion—but just a minute or two to listen. . . .

She talked numbly and steadily until we boarded the plane, then found her seat in another section. As I hung up my coat, I heard her plaintive voice say to her seat companion, "I'll bet it's cold in Chicago."

I prayed, "Please, God let her listen."*

*Erma Bombeck, *If Life Is a Bowl of Cherries—What Am I Doing in the Pits?* (New York: McGraw-Hill, 1978), 197–98.

QUESTION: What makes it difficult for you to really be present and listen when someone talks to you?

CHALLENGE: Who has God put in your life who might need someone to listen to them? Give that person a phone call. Simply say that God put them on your heart, and you wanted to check in and see how they're doing. Then listen and ask follow-up questions when appropriate. You don't need to have any great answers at the end. You can just tell your friend you'll pray for them.

listen to God.
listen to people.

JESUS SAID what's most important is:

1. Love God.
2. Love people.

I wonder if much of the time the way we do that best is:

1. Listen to God.
2. Listen to people.

I sometimes think listening is almost the whole ball game. Yeah, there's lots of things I want to say, but if I just listened, it'd open people up to hear me. When I think back, I realize many of my worst moments have been when I didn't care enough to slow down, give someone my full attention, and really listen. And some of my very best moments were those few times when I did stop and listen.

One time I was staying at a hotel and got hungry. There was a restaurant nearby, so I decided to walk to it. A man approached me on the sidewalk and asked if I could spare just a few bucks. I checked my pockets and found I had a wadded-up dollar bill. I handed it to him. "Thanks, man," he said.

I started walking away—I seem to always just walk away, and besides, I had an agenda of my own—but something stopped me. Call it a nudge. I stopped and asked the man, "Would you mind if I asked you a few questions?"

He gave me one of those looks you see on TV when an informer is being questioned: *Yeah, but it's gonna cost you a little more.*

I told him I had no more cash. But he thought about it and decided to cooperate anyway. I guess he had no other place to go.

He told me his name was Lenny. I asked, "Where do you live?"

His eyes moved down the street, then back at me. "You're looking at it."

"Really? It can get cold in this town."

He nodded. "I know a few shelters for the coldest nights."

"So, how long have you been living on the street?"

"I'd say . . ." He stopped and thought. "Eight years."

I asked, "What's the hardest part for you?"

Lenny didn't hesitate. "Asking for help, man. Asking for help."

I was struck by that. No meal could be taken for granted. Weather was a constant threat. He had no real privacy—I could think of lots of hardships he faced. But for him, asking for help was the hardest obstacle of all.

Lenny and I talked a few more minutes. I wouldn't say it changed his life—in fact, I'm sure it didn't—but it changed me. And at least Lenny met someone who was sincerely interested in his life. Remember, as Bonhoeffer wrote, "Often a person can be helped merely by having someone who will listen to him seriously."*

The scary thing to me is that I had all the time in the world that night, but I almost hurried away. Not because I was afraid, but just because I didn't care enough to stop and listen.

Can I share one more quote from Bonhoeffer? In *Life Together*, he warned,

> He who can no longer listen to his brother will soon be no longer listening to God either; he will be doing nothing but prattle in the presence of God too. This is the beginning of the death of the spiritual life. . . . Anyone who thinks that his time is too valuable to spend keeping quiet will eventually have no time for God and his brother, but only for himself and for his own follies.†

*Bonhoeffer, *Life Together*, 99.
†Bonhoeffer, *Life Together*, 97–98.

QUESTION: What do you think about the idea that much of the time the best way to love God and love people is to listen to God and listen to people?

CHALLENGE: What if, the next time you interact with a homeless person, you ask if you can ask them a few questions? You could ask, "Do you live on the street? For how long? What's the hardest part?" Then thank the person for talking to you, and pray for them.

54

eats with sinners

ASK A NON-CHRISTIAN what they assume about Christians. Chances are the answer won't be pleasant. One thing you'd probably hear is, "Christians are judgmental. If I hung out with them, they'd just make me feel bad for my sin."

What's crazy is that everywhere Jesus went, the most sinful people around were drawn to him. Why did sinful people want to be around Jesus? I think it's because Jesus didn't make them feel bad. No one wants to be around someone who makes them feel bad.

Jesus made them feel loved.

Sinners wanted to be around Jesus. I wonder, Do sinful people want to be around you? Are you someone people feel sure will show them compassion and not condemnation?

Not only did sinners want to be around Jesus; he wanted to be around them. In fact, when Jesus encountered someone committed to sinning, his response was to eat with them. That infuriated the religious people. It was their biggest accusation against him.

> Now the tax collectors and sinners were all gathering around to hear Jesus. But the Pharisees and the teachers of the law muttered, "This man welcomes sinners and eats with them." (Luke 15:1–2)

They were exactly right. Jesus *did* welcome sinners and eat with them.

One day, Luke 19 tells us, Jesus walked into the town of Jericho. The most notorious sinner in Jericho was Zacchaeus, a betrayer of God and God's people. At the time, the Romans were taking over the world with violence and oppression. The Roman army would march into a town, demand everyone worship Caesar, and execute those who wouldn't.

The Romans would then recruit a local to be the tax collector. In Jericho, that was Zacchaeus. Zacchaeus, a Jew, sided with the Romans and collected taxes from the Jews to pay for Rome's army so they could go to other towns, make other people worship Caesar, and kill more faithful Jews who refused. If that wasn't enough, Zacchaeus also made the locals give more money than the

Romans required, so he could line his own pockets with the excess.

Question: If Zacchaeus were standing in front of you, what would you say to him?

I can think of some good options. "How could you do this?" "You are Jewish, yet you're with the Romans who are killing the Jewish people. You are complicit in their murders!" "You do realize that by siding with the Romans, you're betraying God? How dare you. Do you know the punishment that's coming for you?"

What did Jesus say to Zacchaeus? "I must stay at your house today" (v. 5). Jesus invited himself over for lunch.

Why?

I think of John 3:17: "God did not send his Son into the world to condemn the world, but to save the world through him." Jesus didn't come with condemnation for sin. He came with compassion to bring down the wall of sin so he could bring people to God.

So, Jesus went to Zacchaeus's home for a meal, and it worked. By dessert, Zacchaeus had repented of his sin and stepped into abundant and eternal life with God.

Breaking bread breaks barriers.

We need to make people feel loved. How do we do that?

One way is one meal at a time.

That's why Jesus ate with sinners. He came to bring people to God. To break down the barrier between God and people. Of course he was going to break bread with them.

And remember, if you choose to follow Jesus, God's will for your life on earth is the same as his will for Jesus's life on earth.

QUESTION: Jesus zoomed in on Zacchaeus and shared a meal with him. Who's your Zacchaeus? Who has God put in your path who is far from him?

CHALLENGE: God's will is for you to bring your "Zacchaeus" to him. That might sound intimidating, so start with a meal. Invite your coworker out to lunch or your neighbor over for dinner. You don't need to have an incredible spiritual conversation that first meal. Enjoy your time together, ask lots of questions, and listen. Then set up a second meal. Your relationship will grow, you'll feel more comfortable with the idea of bringing up Jesus, and eventually you will find opportunities to turn the conversation from superficial to spiritual.

Everything doesn't typically happen in just one meal like it did with Jesus and Zacchaeus, but you never know what one meal can lead to.

55

breaking down the wall

DO YOU REMEMBER the movie *Remember the Titans*?

Coach Herman Boone (played by Denzel Washington) becomes head football coach of a team in a high school just being forced to racially integrate. The black and white players have little to no experience with people of a different race and are full of prejudices. They seem to have no interest in breaking down the barriers that divide them.

So . . .

I want to tell you something about God. God is love, but God hates. There are things God hates because God is love.

God hates when his children, whom he loves, are separated from him. And God hates when his children, whom he loves, are separated from each other.

That's why God sent Jesus. Jesus came to bring people to God *and* to bring people together.

> But now you have been united with Christ Jesus. Once you were far away from God, but now you have been brought near to him through the blood of Christ.
>
> For Christ himself has brought peace to us. He united Jews and Gentiles into one people when, in his own body on the cross, he broke down the wall of hostility that separated us. (Eph. 2:13–14 NLT)

Unfortunately, there are still so many people who are separated from God and from each other.

One wall that separates God's kids is the color of their skin. Studies reveal that the social networks of most people are filled almost exclusively with people who look like them.* Worse, some have misperceptions or suspicions about those of other races. In some cities, as we've seen, this has produced a boiling cauldron of discord and distress.

Jesus came to do away with those divisions and to show us that we truly are all created equal

> There is no longer Jew or Gentile, slave or free, male and female. For you are all one in Christ Jesus. (Gal. 3:28 NLT)

*One way you can kind of evaluate if this is true for you is to look at your first one hundred Facebook friends. How many of them are of the same race as you?

You may have grown up being taught something different, and it can be difficult to overcome what we've always believed. As a Jew, Peter grew up being taught to discriminate against Gentiles. After three years with Jesus, Peter knew he was to treat everyone as equal. And he did—except when important Jewish people were around. He worried what they might think about him being friends with Gentiles. So he stopped eating with Gentiles.

Paul, another of the early Christians leaders, witnessed Peter's racist behavior and described what happened in his letter to the church in Galatia.

> But when Peter came to Antioch, I had to oppose him to his face, for what he did was very wrong. When he first arrived, he ate with the Gentile believers. . . . But afterward, when some friends of James came, Peter wouldn't eat with the Gentiles anymore. He was afraid of criticism from these people. . . . As a result, other Jewish believers followed Peter's hypocrisy. . . . When I saw that they were not following the truth of the gospel message, I said to Peter in front of all the others, "Since you, a Jew by birth, have discarded the Jewish laws and are living like a Gentile, why are you now trying to make these Gentiles follow the Jewish traditions?" (Gal. 2:11–14 NLT)

Paul said that what Peter was doing—acting like people of his own race were better than others—was "very wrong," "hypocrisy," and "not following the truth of the gospel message."

Paul opposed Peter to his face because what Peter was doing was sin. If you believe your race or your nationality is better than another, that's sin, and you need to repent.

It's interesting to me that Paul's biggest issue with Peter was that he wouldn't eat with people of another race. Meals are so powerful. They can divide, as they did here, but they can also unite.

Remember the racially divided team Coach Boone takes over in *Remember the Titans*? The coach knows a divided team cannot win. But how can he break down the barriers? One day at lunch he has the only white player who eats with black players stand up. He asks this white player questions about a black teammate. Turns out the kid knows about his black teammates. Why? He's eaten with them. Coach Boone then tells the team that everyone will interview players of the other race—they are to ask questions and listen.

That's a great plan. Eat together. Ask questions. Listen.

QUESTION: What is a race of people you don't know much about or might have some prejudices against?

CHALLENGE: Set up a meal with someone who is different from you.

If you don't have a close friend from another race, who could you ask from that race to go out for a meal? What if

you told them, very humbly, that you want to better understand what it's like to be someone who is not you? What if
you asked them if they would share their story, some truths
about their race, and if they've had any experiences with
racism?

WEEK 12

the practice of
serving

[one need at a time]

choose love

WE'RE GETTING CLOSE to the end of this book. This is the last section. And I have a guess. Here it is: you have no issue with what I've asked you to do in this book.

Serving others? Yeah, who would be against that?

Loving people? Sure, I love love!

Connecting with people so they can connect with God? Yes, please!

You probably haven't taken issue with what I've asked you to do—but you *do* have an issue with actually doing it. This issue is your agenda.

See, connecting with people, loving and influencing them, is always about meeting their needs. That might sound great, but those needs come as an interruption to our own agendas, and there may be nothing like our agendas that keeps us from loving.

If we're going to love like Jesus loved, it'll require a willingness to prioritize the needs of one person at a time above our own agendas. But when we give up our priorities for God's by choosing love, we discover that it's always the right trade.

One day I got a call about an elderly lady, Paulette, who had visited our church one time and wanted me to come visit her at home. That might sound like a reasonable request to make of a pastor, but we have a very large church and it's impossible for me to show up at everyone's house. However, I was told Paulette didn't have much time left to live. To be honest, the timing couldn't have been worse. I looked at my calendar to find when it might be possible, but there were no options.

I would've just said no, but I'd committed myself to connecting with people one at a time. I cursed myself for making that stupid commitment and said I'd get to her home somehow.

I learned that before Paulette's one visit to our church, she hadn't been to church since she was a young girl. Now, barring a miracle, she was dying of pancreatic cancer, and hospice had been called in.

When I walked in I was greeted by her husband, who was of a different faith. He challenged me, "Give me thirty days, and I'll convert you." I liked him right away.

He walked me into the living room where Paulette was in her wheelchair. I sat down and shared the gospel with her. I told her that, like me, she was a sinner. Her husband wasn't sure about that, insisting that she was an extraordinary woman. I explained that the punishment we deserve for our sins is death. I shared the Good News that

Jesus came to die for our sins, to take our punishment on himself. That forgiveness and grace are God's free gift to us when we repent of our sins and put our trust in Jesus as Lord and Savior.

Tears rolled down her cheeks. She said, "I just wish it wasn't too late for me. I had my chance, but it's been too many years. I just wish it wasn't too late."

My eyes filled with tears too. I told her, "Oh, I have some great news. It's never too late."

She prayed with me, and later that evening she was baptized. In fact, it wasn't just Paulette; her daughter and granddaughter were also baptized that night.

Looking back, I'm trying to remember what I had on my calendar that week that seemed so important. I literally have no clue. I'm sure there was work and some meetings; I have lots of those. I just can't believe I almost put whatever was on my agenda above God's agenda. I almost missed the chance to meet Paulette and share Jesus with her because of . . . I have no idea.

Loving people pretty much always means meeting a need, and those needs pretty much always present themselves as interruptions to your agenda. When you're faced with that choice, choose love. You'll be glad you did.

QUESTION: Think back on the last few weeks. When has your agenda kept you from loving someone? When did a person have a need you could meet but didn't because you had something else to do?

CHALLENGE: What is one thing you could take off your calendar this week to free up time to serve someone else in some way? If something doesn't immediately come to mind, pray about it. Then do it!

DAY **57**

small is the new big

I'M NOT A BIG FAN of small. Generally, I prefer big.

Would I like a petite steak or a massive steak? The bigger one, please.

You're slicing my birthday cake? Oh, do I want a sliver or a real piece? Bigger, please.

And the day they stopped offering to super-size my fries? That was a dark day, my friend.

We tend not to think much of "small," and I wonder if that sometimes keeps us from serving others. What we can do for them feels small, and therefore insignificant, and so we wonder if it's even worth it.

Do you ever feel that way? When you see the homeless person who just wants a dollar? When your chronically dismayed coworker just needs someone who's willing to listen . . . again? When you're making brownies for your family and the idea hits you to make a second tray for your difficult neighbors? When the person sitting next to you on the airplane asks a question and you realize you could turn the conversation from superficial to spiritual, but there are only a few minutes left in the flight? Will it really make a difference?

Too often the issue isn't that the need is intimidatingly big, it's that it feels insignificantly small. You can do it, but would it matter?

The answer?

That's not for us to decide. We trust God to use whatever we're able to offer. He's pretty good at making a big impact with something small. I mean, he fed thousands with a kid's sack lunch. I love this quote by Mother Teresa: "Don't look for big things, just do small things with great love."*

When I've thought about people who have met a need of mine, I've realized they probably don't even remember doing it because it didn't seem like a big deal to them—but it was to me.

In eighth grade my Sunday school teacher, Scott Fields, asked me to stay after class. After everyone left, he looked me in the eye and said, "I just want to tell you I think God's really going to use you in your life. I think you are a world-changer."

*As quoted in Brian Kolodiejchuk, ed., *Mother Teresa: Come Be My Light: The Private Writings of the Saint of Calcutta* (New York: Doubleday, 2007), 34.

What he didn't know is the day before, my baseball coach had spit tobacco on my shoes and told me I was worthless. It only took Mr. Fields a few minutes to talk to me. He probably didn't think it would make much difference—but I've never forgotten it.

Back when I was a church intern, my wife and I had less than zero dollars. Someone came up to me the weekend before Valentine's Day and put a hundred-dollar bill in my hand, smiled, and said, "Hey, make your wife feel special." It meant so much to us.

There was the time we wanted to have our basement painted before some relatives came into town, but money was too tight. While we were out of town, our small group broke into our house and painted our basement.

A few years ago, I met for lunch with an elder of our church because I needed to share a personal struggle. I leaned in, and tears came into my eyes as I started to share. He stood up. I wondered, *Uh oh. What's happening?* He walked over to my side of the booth, said, "Scoot over," and sat down next to me. I realized he wanted me to know he was on my side as he listened and prayed for me.

You have no idea of the impact of small things done with great love.

QUESTION: Is there something you haven't done for someone because it feels small? Writing a thank-you note to someone who invested in your life in the past? Making cookies for your neighbor? Writing some sweet little notes for your spouse and posting them all over your house? Texting a friend who's hurting, "I'm sorry for what you're going through, and I'm going to pray for you for the next couple minutes"?

CHALLENGE: Whatever that small thing is, do it—with great love.

compassion
fatigue

IF WE'RE SERIOUS about this one at a time life, I need to warn you about compassion fatigue.

Picture yourself walking down a path. You see another guy walking, and he's carrying thirty pounds of rocks. You offer to take five pounds for him. You start walking again but still feel bad, so you take another five pounds of his burden.

You're doing all right with the ten pounds, but then you see a woman who is struggling to walk with what must be forty pounds of rocks. You take fifteen pounds off of her.

You walk almost a mile and then come across an elderly man who is unable to move because his arms are loaded with heavy rocks. You grab a bunch from his pile. You start to walk again but realize you now have almost fifty pounds, and you just can't do it. You plop down on the side of the path, exhausted.

That's a picture of compassion fatigue. Instead of rocks, we take on the burden of suffering from others because of our Christlike compassion. That's exactly what we're supposed to do: "Carry each other's burdens, and in this way you will fulfill the law of Christ" (Gal. 6:2).

But if you continue to care for the hurting, you can get to a point where it feels like too much. You become tired, you start to feel a darkness, and it becomes very difficult to empathize with others. You just don't have the strength to give compassion anymore.

Psychologists describe four common stages of compassion fatigue:

1. The zealot phase. You're committed to giving compassion!
2. The irritability phase. You start to lose some energy and passion for helping others and become more annoyed with the neediness of people.
3. The withdrawal phase. You're tired and begin avoiding people who may need your help.
4. The zombie phase. You become disconnected from your feelings. You no longer find yourself able to empathize with hurting people.*

*Char Richard, "Compassion Fatigue Scale," June 9, 2013, Charlene Richard RSW, https://www.charlenerichardrsw.com/2013/06/compassion-fatigue-2/.

Remember when Jesus was teaching thousands of people and his disciples told him to send the crowds away so they could go get food? I wonder if the disciples' desire to send the people away wasn't just about food. Is it possible the disciples were feeling some compassion fatigue?

Jesus told them, "Nah. Let's not send them away. You guys feed them." They were probably thinking, *What?!* "Bro, there are . . . maybe fifteen *thousand* people. We did not bring grills. There are no KFC big bucket family specials at the moment. How are we going to feed them?"

Their objections may have felt legitimate. But, as you're probably aware, Jesus miraculously fed all those thousands of people with a kid's sack lunch. The disciples were shocked. They immediately started making cell phones and invented texting so they could send "mind blown" emojis to all their friends.

Then, in the very next chapter, there's *another* full college basketball arena–size hungry crowd on another mountain, and Jesus once again made his disciples aware of the issue. This time they *knew* Jesus had an all-you-can-eat, fast-delivery-take out trick up his sleeve. So, naturally, you just know this time they'd say, "Trick me once—I look silly in Matthew 14. Trick me twice and I'll look *stupid* in Matthew 15. Jesus, you *can't* trick me twice. *We* can feed them!"

Nope. That's not what they said. Instead, "His disciples answered, 'Where could we get enough bread in this remote place to feed such a crowd?'" (Matt. 15:33).

Oh, c'mon. Were they serious? They obviously knew exactly where. Jesus made bread like Taylor Swift makes hit records.

They knew. I think they just didn't want to do it again. They were tired. It's exhausting to distribute food to thousands of people. I think they might've had compassion fatigue. Maybe they felt like they'd already given all they had. There was nothing left.

So, what do you do if you've cared to capacity and your compassion tank is empty? The same thing you do when your car is out of gas. You fill up.

Look what Jesus did immediately after his first *Great Jesus Baking Show* miraculous feeding of the masses: "After he had dismissed them, he went up on a mountainside by himself to pray" (14:23).

Remember the first "one at a time" Jesus story we looked at together? The woman who had been bleeding for years snuck up and swiped a miracle by touching Jesus's cloak. Jesus knew it happened. How? He said, "Someone touched me; I know that power has gone out from me" (Luke 8:46).

When Jesus served people, power went out of him.

When *you* serve someone, it'll take something out of you too.

But Jesus kept serving—he overcame compassion fatigue—by getting alone with God so he could be filled back up.

We need to do that too. Remember, the secret sauce is in then through.

QUESTION: Earlier in the book we talked about prioritizing your relationship with God and your plan for spiritual growth. How is that going?

CHALLENGE: Your challenge today is just to sit quietly in God's presence and breathe. Breathe in God's love. Ask him to (re)fill you.

59

rejection
therapy

YOU HAVE BEEN PRESENTED with a ton of challenges in this book. Fifty-eight of them so far, to be exact. I suspect that a bunch of them raised some fear. You may be putting off some because you're nervous.

Afraid of what? Probably rejection.

Am I right?

If you are going to invite someone over for dinner or to a party, or offer to serve a person, or try to start a spiritual conversation, there's a fear: *What if they reject me?*

We need to overcome that fear.

Did you hear about Jia Jiang? Jia grew up with a debilitating fear of rejection. As a young adult, he had dreams for his life and career, but he would never do what needed to be done to achieve them, because he was always afraid.

Stuck and miserable, one day he googled, "How do I overcome the fear of rejection?" He came across the theory of rejection therapy. The idea is that you intentionally get rejected every day, once a day. Eventually, rejection therapy says, you'll be desensitized from the pain of rejection. Voila! No more fear.

Jia decided, *What's the worst that could happen?*

He came up with a hundred ideas he knew would receive rejection and got to work, one day at a time.

Day one: ask a stranger for $100. He made the request but ran away before the guy could answer.

Day two: request a "burger refill." He went to a restaurant, ate his burger, and then asked the employee at the counter to refill his burger. The guy asked, "What?!" Jia said, "I ate my burger. Can I have another one?" The guy laughed. "I don't think we do that."

Jia was rejected, but he realized it didn't feel so bad.

Day three: get Olympic doughnuts. Jia went to a Krispy Kreme and asked them to interlink five doughnuts and make them the colors of the Olympic rings. He knew they'd say no. Except they said yes.*

From that day on, Jia kept asking, still seeking rejection—but he kept getting yesses! He asked if he could:

*Jia recorded his rejection attempts. You can watch the Olympic doughnuts video at "Rejection Therapy Day 3—Ask for Olympic Symbol Doughnuts. Jackie at Krispy Kreme Delivers!" YouTube video, 2:22 uploaded by Jia Jiang, November 18, 2012, https://www.youtube.com/watch?v=7Ax2CsVbrX0.

Plant a flower in a stranger's backyard. Yes!

Be the "Walmart greeter"—at a Starbucks. Yes!

Give a weather forecast on live TV. Yes!

Sit in the driver's seat of a police car. Yes!

Make his own sandwich at a Subway. Yes!

He got a yes for *everything*, and he overcame his fear of rejection.* Jia Jiang learned that his fear was unfounded.

And *you* don't need to fear.

Why?

First, because people are way more open to you—to your invitations, your words, your care for them—than you think they are.

Second, you don't need to fear because the reward is worth the risk. Let's say you start living a one at a time life, and so over the next few years you invite twenty people over for meals or parties, and you offer to do some act of service for twenty people, and you initiate spiritual conversations with twenty people. What if you get rejected by two of the twenty people you invite and two you offer to serve and two you talk to? That might sting a little, but you would have *fifty-four* people whom you'd influenced for Jesus! I bet some of their lives would be changed.

*Jia Jiang also did a TED Talk on his rejection therapy journey. See Jia Jiang, "What I Learned from 100 Days of Rejection," TED Talk, 15:23, TEDxMtHood, May 2015, https://www.ted.com/talks/jia_jiang_what _i_learned_from_100_days_of_rejection?language=en.

Would that be worth it? Of course it would!

And third, you don't need to fear because God has told you to *fear not*. Over three hundred times in the Bible, God tells you not to fear. You can go serve and meet needs and invite without fear of rejection. Be emboldened by these words from God:

> I said, "You are my servant";
>> I have chosen you and have not rejected you.
> So do not fear, for I am with you;
>> do not be dismayed, for I am your God.
>> I will strengthen you and help you;
> I will uphold you with my righteous right hand.
>> (Isa. 41:9–10)

QUESTION: What fears do you have about living a one at a time kind of life? Think about those fears in this way: What's the worst that could happen? In reality, how bad would it be?

CHALLENGE: Memorize Isaiah 41:9–10 and use it to fight against fear.

60

God's answer is me

WE'RE AT THE END of this book and at the start of a new life. We have started living in the one at a time way of Jesus. The question is, Will we continue in it?

Why should we continue? I have a few reasons for you.

The first reason has to do with a skunk.

Elizabeth Sherrill was working on her computer one afternoon when she saw a skunk stumble across her yard wearing a yellow helmet.

Well, it looked like a helmet but it was actually a plastic yogurt container. The container was stuck on its head, and it was frantically trying to get loose. Elizabeth thought, *Someone needs to help that skunk. Surely someone will come along.* But no one did, so she called the wildlife department, thinking they would send someone out.

They wouldn't. They told Elizabeth that *she* needed to pull the yogurt container off the skunk's head.

"What if it sprays me?" she asked.

"If a skunk can't see you, it won't spray you."

"Yeah, but what happens when the carton comes off?"

"Make sure it doesn't feel threatened," they advised.

She went out into her yard, then saw the skunk running right toward her. She knelt down, grabbed the yogurt container, and yanked it off. Elizabeth found herself staring into the skunk's beady eyes. Then it turned and ran away.

Later, Elizabeth wrote about her encounter with the apparently yogurt-loving skunk, "I thought . . . the skunk was all those needs I hesitate to get involved in. . . . Somebody else can handle it better. . . . But . . . every now and then, God's answer to a need . . . is me."*

There are so many people God loves out there. They have a lot of needs. You're not responsible to meet all of them, but you are responsible for some. Every now and then, God's answer to a need is you.

The second reason to continue in this life has to do with Batman.

When my kids were young, my wife would go out in early November and buy costumes, as stores practically give them away after Halloween, for the kids to use for

*Nageshwar Das, "Skunk on the Loose," I Learn Lot, February 20, 2017, https://www.ilearnlot.com/skunk-on-the-loose/1325/.

God's answer is me

playing dress-up. She would choose superhero costumes for my son. Why? Because he wanted to be a superhero, of course. One costume was Batman, and when I opened it I noticed it had a warning on it. It said: "Warning: Cape does not enable user to fly." I'm serious. In other words, "Hey, kid, have fun pretending to be Batman, but don't get too carried away with this."

Don't you want to be a hero? *Hero* may be a strong word, but I think we all want to make a real difference with our lives. But it's easy to think, *Who am I? I need to temper my aspirations. I shouldn't get carried away.*

Yes, you should.

I love the "Hall of Fame" of the heroes of the faith in Hebrews 11. It's filled with the stories of people who did amazing things for God. *People.* Not superheroes. People. Normal people like you. Normal people who lived by faith in an *amazing* God. That's what led and empowered them to do such amazing things. And you can join these heroes of the faith. Just trust God and do whatever he calls you to do.

The third reason to continue in this life has to do with stickers.

When I was a kid growing up in Sunday school, we were rewarded for doing well. There was a chart on our classroom wall that had categories like, "Church attendance," "Bring a Bible," "Put in the offering," and "Invite a friend." If you did one, you got a sticker! Instant reward.

Not today. There's no instant reward. But reward *is* coming. We're encouraged in Galatians 6:9, "Let us not become weary in doing good, for at the proper time we will reap a harvest if we do not give up."

We don't serve and love others selfishly, for the reward. But it is encouraging to know reward is coming. And I love that the reward mentioned in Galatians 6:9 is "a harvest." We won't get a sticker, but we will get a harvest.

Sometimes I feel like I'm trying to do good, but I'm not seeing any result. Do you ever feel that way? Well, be patient. Trust God. Keep connecting with and loving people, one at a time.

A harvest is coming.

QUESTION: Where right now do you feel like God's answer is *you*? What need in someone's life has he positioned you to meet? Who can you serve?

CHALLENGE: Put Galatians 6:9 on a card or on a note on your phone. Commit to reading it every morning.

Kyle Idleman is senior pastor at Southeast Christian Church in Louisville, Kentucky, one of the ten largest churches in America, where he speaks to more than thirty thousand people each weekend. He is the best-selling and award-winning author of *Not a Fan* as well as *One at a Time*, *gods at war*, and *Don't Give Up*. He is a frequent speaker for national conventions and in influential churches across the country. Kyle and his wife, DesiRae, have four children and live on a farm, where he doesn't do any actual farming.

connect with
KYLE

f @kyleidleman @kyleidleman

kyleidleman.com

The Secret to Being a Difference-Maker?
Loving People One at a Time.

With conviction and humor, bestselling author Kyle Idleman challenges true disciples to fully commit to the unexpected, Jesus way of changing the world: by loving people one at a time. He helps us understand Jesus's surprising habits, unlock the power of small things done with great love, and discover how God wants to use us to change the world one person at a time.

God-Sized Courage for When You Are at the End of Your Rope

"Encouragement to keep believing, keep fighting, and keep perspective. If you need to find your courage and strength in the midst of life's challenges, this book is for you."

—Dr. Kevin Leman, *New York Times* bestselling author of *Have a New Kid by Friday*

Experience God's Amazing Gift of Grace

"By the end of this book you will see grace in a new light; you will see your loving God in a new light. Read it and be encouraged."

—Max Lucado, author of *GRACE* and *In the Grip of Grace*

BakerBooks
a division of Baker Publishing Group
www.BakerBooks.com

Available wherever books and ebooks are sold.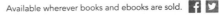